BECOMING
DATA
LITERATE

T0347686

Every owner of a physical copy of this edition of

BECOMING
DATA
LITERATE

can download the eBook for free direct from us at
Harriman House, in a DRM-free format that can be read
on any eReader, tablet or smartphone.

Simply head to:

ebooks.harriman-house.com/becomingdataliterate

to get your copy now.

BECOMING DATA LITERATE

Building a great business,
culture and leadership through
data and analytics

DAVID REED

Foreword by Adrian Gregory,
Co-founder and CEO, DataIQ

HARRIMAN HOUSE LTD
3 Viceroy Court
Bedford Road
Petersfield
Hampshire
GU32 3LJ
GREAT BRITAIN
Tel: +44 (0)1730 233870

Email: enquiries@harriman-house.com
Website: harriman.house

First published in 2021.

Paperback ISBN: 978-0-85719-927-0
eBook ISBN: 978-0-85719-928-7

British Library Cataloguing in Publication Data
A CIP catalogue record for this book can be obtained from the British Library.

Contents

Foreword

I would be lying if I said I was passionate about data. My passion is business, specifically helping people in business who drive performance, especially when they use data to achieve success. I love what data can achieve when used intelligently.

Successful businesses create. They create opportunities, wealth, jobs and careers, relationships, solutions to problems and, most of all as a combined economic force, businesses create growth and progress.

To prosper today demands being data-driven. As Silicon Valley has shown with the success of Amazon, Apple, Facebook and Google, this is how prominent market positions and remarkable valuations are created.

But established firms are fighting back. In 2021, for the third consecutive year, 99% of firms in the Fortune 1000 are investing in data and artificial intelligence (AI) according to research by New Vantage Partners published in the *Harvard Business Review*.

However, while these data capabilities continue to accelerate, very few are delivering the anticipated results, the *Harvard Business Review* reported in February 2021. This is very much in line with our own research findings and experiences with the global, FTSE 100, large- and mid-market organisations that make up the DataIQ community.

Why is this? You will find many of the reasons called out in this book, but a major issue that needs to be addressed is legacy culture, especially a lack of focus on people and their soft skills, including the ability to communicate key data insights to non-data experts in senior management. It is this important step that leads towards developing successful data-driven businesses. Real-world examples from Aviva, GSK, Jaguar Land Rover and Zurich show how established firms are able to overcome these obstacles and pursue their visions.

DataIQ has taken the success factors we have seen time and again from companies like these and developed them into a framework for building a truly data-driven business – we call it the DataIQ Way.

It starts with the fundamental importance of aligning the organisation's broader vision and strategy with its data vision and strategy, and proceeds with building leadership, skills and culture – focusing on people, not technology. To compete and prosper, businesses need to become truly data literate and speak the language of data throughout the business, hence the title of the book.

The DataIQ Way is heavily evidence-based, built on years of hands-on experience working with established global, FTSE 100, large- and mid-market enterprises, combined with extensive research, and in-depth interviews with over 600 industry leaders. Throughout, it is based on practical experience rather than textbook theories.

My own love for data started in the early 1980s. As a young, impressionable marketing consultant, I first got excited about what was then called direct marketing and the potential it offered to drive sales and business growth. I visited one of the leading marketing agencies at the time, Ogilvy Direct, and picked up in reception a bright red brochure which simply said on the front, "Never sell to a stranger". I loved it!

The theme, of course, was all about collecting and analysing data on consumers and from this understanding, sending them relevant messages to win their confidence and convert them to customers. It became known as one-to-one marketing, then data or database marketing and, more recently, data-driven marketing – we work in an industry built on buzz words!

Excited by the opportunities in data and with a passion for business, I set up the first of my five data-centric businesses in October 1988 and stayed with it right through its rapid growth in the second decade of this century. As often as this saw positive data usage and business growth, it also involved misuse and rogue operators. It was to combat this that I started DQM Group, out of which DataIQ launched in 2011.

I have known David Reed, this book's author, since the late 1980s and saw in his journalism the same interest in data – and maintaining standards – as I felt. His communication skills have allowed us to attract, develop and engage with our ever-expanding community of data and analytics professionals. I would like to thank David for the considerable work involved in researching and writing this book on top of his day job, and even more for the ten years we have worked together at DataIQ helping our members and the broader DataIQ community.

And it is people – data leaders and data practitioners – that make the real difference. Their expertise in applying technology and techniques to raw data, combined with an ability to communicate findings effectively, that allows their organisations to harness the power of data, transform their businesses and create truly great data literate businesses.

A growing number of organisations are on this journey, many of them still at the early stages. We are confident that by focusing on the methods and framework detailed in this book, you'll be able to fast-track your own progress to data-driven success and even become a great business.

Adrian Gregory
Co-founder and CEO
DataIQ

Introduction:
Towards evidence-based
decision-making

"The substance of things hoped for. The evidence of things not seen."

– Hebrews 11.1

I N 1999, THE then Health Secretary in the UK government, Frank Dobson, wanted to understand the balance between cost and effectiveness of drugs prescribed by the National Health Service (NHS). Typically, decisions about prescribing were being made at a local, rather than national level, creating a culture of 'postcode prescribing' with differences in the treatments available across the country.

Wanting a change in approach to make delivery consistent everywhere, he appointed Sir Andrew Dillon to be the first chief executive of the National Institute for Clinical Excellence (now NICE – National Institute for Health and Care Excellence), who set about appraising widely prescribed drugs for their benefit to patients and costs to the NHS.

It was the birth of evidence-based decision-making in healthcare and a model for what the data industry is currently trying to achieve in the commercial realm. Instead of leaving each stakeholder to decide based on their own experience and intuition, end-to-end data on options through to outcomes is assembled, analysed and modelled to reveal patterns and insights. These can then be used to support decision-making and, in the process, often transform the choices that are made.

As NICE discovered early on, data-driven decision-making can be controversial. Its first ever recommendation was that the NHS should stop prescribing Relenza, an antiviral treatment for flu, because it did little to reduce the impact of the illness on high-risk groups, such as the elderly and asthmatic. Mike Thompson, chief executive of the Association of the British Pharmaceutical Industry, commented on this decision: "That was the day that the world changed forever for the pharmaceutical industry and I think companies got it."

Data leaders may feel that they stand on the brink of their own world-changing moment as they build out their data offices and seek to build levels of data literacy across the organisation. In view is a transformation of the strategies, decisions, processes and value that can be realised. But there are many obstacles to overcome, from political resistance and entrenched cultures through to data silos and technology debt. To a leadership that was appointed for its technical abilities and with the tailwind of advocacy for data – created by terms such as the 'Fourth Industrial Revolution', for example – these can seem insurmountable and outside of personal competence and skillset.

The DataIQ Way has been built as a framework to guide data leaders on this journey. As this book outlines, there are actions, issues and resolutions that can be linked together to form a pathway towards data literacy and a true data culture, including evidence-based decision-making by the senior executive downwards.

Our approach is itself evidence-based. Since launch in 2011, DataIQ has published over 1,500 articles and news stories which have told the story of data's growth during the 'golden decade' of interest and investment. It is worth noting that until 2012, the term 'big data' was still the preserve of life sciences and cloud computing was viewed with suspicion by IT departments – a far cry from the current situation in which the UK government has developed a National Data Strategy to reap the benefits of this resource.

We have carried more than 800 profiles of data leaders in the DataIQ 100, our list of the most influential people in data that debuted in 2014. That same year saw the launch of the DataIQ Awards, which have attracted in excess of 600 entries to date. Our research programme has solicited responses from nearly 3,500 data practitioners as part of 24 survey pulses. Since the launch in 2017 of our membership service, DataIQ Leaders, we have had over 30 group discussions lasting some 100 hours with the most senior figures in the data industry and have welcomed some 700 data practitioners to our workshops. Through the DataIQ Podcast, we have also carried out deep dives with more than 40 data leaders.

This author has been involved across all of these activities, gaining as a result a profound understanding of the role data is playing in every sector and scale of organisation. The synthesis of this knowledge is presented in this book, while practical support based on this framework is now available to our membership.

For the NHS – and the UK population as a whole – the pay-off from the shift to evidence-based decision-making was very clear when the Covid-19 pandemic broke. Close links had grown up between academia and the life sciences sector through this shared mindset and research-based approach to pharmaceutical development. As a result, an accelerated vaccine programme allowed the UK medicines regulator to be presented with early-stage evidence and recognise that the tests involved had been properly structured and that the vaccine production process could prove its safety. This led to the country being able to vaccinate the population at a faster rate than countries within the European Union. It has also led to the creation of the role of national director of data and analytics in NHS England – a clear indicator that the culture of seeking evidence is now formalised in healthcare.

We believe that publication of this book ushers in the day when commercial organisations experience a similar fundamental change as senior executives finally recognise the central role data can play and the transformation in their culture it will bring about.

CHAPTER I
Laying data foundations

Roadmap – in this chapter:

- Data integration can appear too expensive for individual projects to afford.

- If multiple projects need to draw on the data asset, they can be 'taxed' to pay for it.

- Without integrated data, value-creating projects will stall.

- Data quality is another obstacle that can cost 8.8% of annual revenue.

- Data technology is becoming a commodity – more affordable, but providing less competitive advantage.

Technology is not the transformer

Crossing the data bridge

B ACK IN 2018, the chief data officer (CDO) of a telco giant recognised the opportunity that existed from monetising anonymised, aggregated location data. As a tool for developing and supporting services as well as for the targeting of marketing messages based on retail proximity, mobile data has unsurpassed coverage and depth.

But there was a problem. Data silos existed right across the business, which had grown through acquisition as much as organically. Data management had tended to be an afterthought and was under-invested. While the business case for putting location data into the marketplace was compelling, it would require significant upfront investment into data integration with year one costs in excess of expected revenues. This made getting buy-in from the executive a real challenge.

As many data leaders have discovered for themselves, despite the impetus behind data as a transformational asset and the widespread advocacy for adopting data and analytics, it can be a struggle to get their investment case approved. This is because of the point of view that, 'the first person to cross the river pays for the bridge'. What this means is that the full cost of a data project, such as a major data integration, is often imposed on the first new business project which needs it, be that a digital transformation or a new data product.

So how can the CDO get around this obstacle? The approach taken at that telco was to build up a fund by including an incremental levy or data tax on all business projects in the run-up to and during digital transformations. Just like the tolls paid by traffic to cross a real bridge and thereby pay for the cost of its construction, gaining smaller contributions towards a larger project means that no single business process or department leader is left facing the whole bill. This can also establish the data office as a stand-alone function with cross-functional support from within the business, giving it greater independence and resilience.

Accelerating growth of digital technology and its adoption by organisations, governments and consumers will be the indisputable trend of the 2020s. As part of this, data is moving from being a simple raw material that fuels these technologies to being a form of digital currency – the price of operating in the digital space at any level is the supply of data in some form.

For companies that want to thrive – and more pressingly for those which hope to survive – during the 2020s, rapid adoption and maturity of data and analytics capabilities is therefore fundamental. This was already recognised in the 2010s when data-led transformation was just getting underway under the badge of 'big data'.

In a landmark report by Nesta, the UK's innovation foundation, published in 2014 under the title, *Inside the Datavores*, the authors noted: "We find that a one-standard deviation greater use of online data is associated with an 8% higher level of productivity – firms in the top quartile of online data use are, other things being equal, 13% more productive than those in the bottom quartile. When we distinguish between the different data-related activities that firms undertake, we find that greater data analysis and reporting of data insights have the strongest link with productivity, whereas *amassing data has little or no effect on its own*."

Firms have taken notice of this and investment into data foundations is now a differentiator between leaders and laggards across most sectors. As the UK's National Data Strategy spelled out in 2020: "Poor data foundations can be a real blocker for driving the transformative power of data. For example, when the source data needed to power AI or machine learning is not fit for purpose, it leads to poor or inaccurate results, and to delays in realising the benefits of innovation."

Growth can be driven by taking the first steps into data and analytics, especially if transforming from a very low, immature base. The economic argument for doing so is virtually irresistible and can often be made by focusing on fixing the data foundations ahead of innovating and value creation.

As an example of this, the digital transformation of the Lloyd's of London insurance market is expected to remove £800 million in operating costs, equal to 3% of its current total operating costs, with a core data store being built to support digital processing. Its roadmap, Blueprint Two, spells this out clearly: "The transformation envisaged is only possible if complete, accurate and timely data is available to support and connect digital processes. It is the quality of this data that makes the difference between an automated process that happens immediately and a manual process that routinely takes days today."

Similarly, Lorenzo Bavasso, data, analytics and AI director at BT Global, states: "We have to move towards data foundations that are defined/built for every business function to define their data-driven plans and execute them. Also, the funding approach has to evolve from central/use case-based business cases to a model where the core capability is built as a fundamental need of the business and then exploited (value-driven) across the business, with a degree of autonomy."

Another common basis for the investment case into data foundations is to fix issues with poor data quality. Unless concerted attempts are made to resolve these, they can have an ongoing and direct impact on turnover by increasing costs (through customer service overheads or logistics failures) or decreasing revenue (through lost customers, sales and opportunities).

As Figure 1.1 shows, this negative impact continues to rise, hitting an average of 8.8% of annual revenue in 2020 compared to an average of 5.6% in 2017. This not only flags that data quality can be an evergreen thorn in the side of the organisation, but it also presents a risk – fines for violations of the General Data Protection Regulation (GDPR) in the EU (or Data Protection Act (DPA) in the UK) can reach 4% of global turnover. A clear link can be made between errors and gaps in data and the ability of an organisation to know whether its data has been breached.

Figure 1.1: Average annual cost of poor-quality data

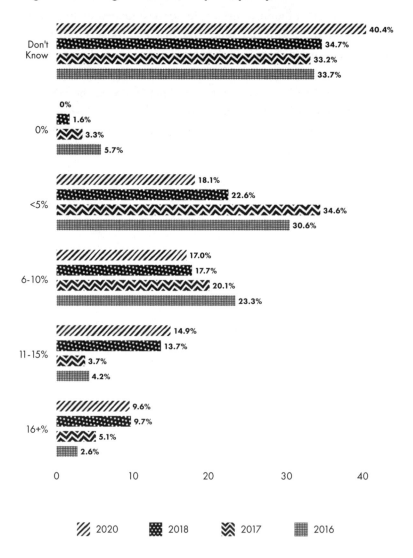

Pens, pencils and winning the (space) race

Given the need to put data foundations in place, it can be tempting to view data technology as both the fix for existing problems and also the heart of a digital transformation. But technology rarely achieves the second of these goals in its own right, as a story from the early days of the space race helps to illustrate.

NASA discovered it faced a technical challenge – astronauts needed to be able to write and carry out calculations, but conventional pens would not work in an environment where the temperature could swing between minus 50 degrees Fahrenheit and plus 400 degrees. So it invested millions of dollars into R&D to come up with specially engineered space pens. Meanwhile, the Russian space programme simply gave its cosmonauts pencils.

It's a story to gladden the heart of any financial director, speaking as it does to thrift and the avoidance of over-engineered solutions. Widely told, this example is often given as a cautionary tale about seeing technology as the solution without considering alternatives or existing assets.

Unfortunately, it's not true. NASA did overspend on writing tools, buying 34 mechanical pencils from Houston's Tycam Engineering Manufacturing in 1965 for a total of $4,382.50 or $128.89 per pencil. But Russian space travellers did not use regular pencils because they are flammable, could snap during use and create dangerous litter inside a capsule.

The reality of how writing in space was tackled is actually more interesting and even more relevant when thinking about investing in data foundations. The private company Fisher Pens invested a reported $1 million to develop a patented space pen that worked in the extreme conditions faced by astronauts and cosmonauts. And it sold these pens to both the Apollo and Soyuz programmes at a cost of just $2.98 each.

Across the data and analytics space, private companies are investing heavily to develop the tools and solutions needed by organisations and provide them as cloud-based or as-a-service products. Just as with space pens, these solutions are available to all-comers at commodity prices.

This makes the creation of strong data foundations more achievable, just as Fisher Pens allowed space travellers to write easily and cheaply. But at the same time, putting these data foundations in place does not confer any competitive advantage in itself since the same technology can be adopted by rivals, start-ups and disruptors.

It is a common misperception that technology in itself provides the fix required. In fact, this is very rarely the case. As we explore in subsequent chapters, it is the shift in culture and the unlocking of a new vision for the business, combined with an alignment between business strategy and data strategy, that ultimately transforms any organisation. Data literacy means understanding how to create a great business with data at its heart, rather than trying to become a data business.

DATA LITERACY STEPCOUNTER

At the end of each chapter in this book, you will find some key steps that we have identified as critical points on the DataIQ Way journey. In the final chapter, we bring these together in the wireframe for your own progression.

Steps 1–3:

1. Fund data foundations progressively to remove financial objections.

2. Use data quality as a cost justification.

3. Recognise that data technology alone does not bring about transformation.

CHAPTER 2
Organising for data and analytics

Roadmap – in this chapter:

- Zurich Insurance UK and Samsung Europe started with specific, constrained goals for data that rapidly grew.

- GSK Consumer Healthcare and Lloyd's of London are putting data at the heart of business transformations.

- Some 83% of organisations are pursuing digital-first transformations.

- Data needs to be organised into its own department – a central data office.

- Reporting lines for the CDO vary widely, but also have a significant impact on the CDO's effectiveness.

- Roles can be defined by the tasks involved – centralisation avoids duplication of effort and conflicts of view.

- Standardisation of roles is lacking in the data industry, leading to over-demand and salary inflation.

Vision

Recognising the vision gap

IN 2018, ZURICH Insurance UK recognised it had a data problem. A complex and fragmented data estate had grown up covering over 20 separate legacy systems. Management information (MI) had become sprawling and uncoordinated with over 400 processes being supported and extensive legacy reports being produced. As Anita Fernqvist, CDO and director of operations at Zurich Insurance UK, recalls: "Data had become a major issue for the organisation that needed focus, dedication and investment and, due to my delivery track record, I was asked to take up the challenge. In year one, I carried out a data deep dive, proposed a strategy and created a data architecture and analytics function, securing significant investment for delivery. By year two, we had put live the first phase of our strategic data asset and laid firm foundations for becoming a truly data-centric organisation, with year three significantly maturing the asset and the benefits flowing into the organisation."

Driven by the problems this lack of data integration was causing for its property and casualty market managers, Zurich Insurance UK recruited Fernqvist as its first CDO within its then data architecture and analytics (DAA) team, supported by a team of ten. Working across data architecture, data quality, DevOps and portfolio management, the team rapidly grew to 30 (and subsequently several hundred). Their goal was to revolutionise the way data was stored and used through the creation of a strategic data asset as an enabler of a mindset shift – from viewing data as a risk to giving it a voice in the boardroom and becoming a key decision-making support.

A data strategy, roadmap and operating model gained sign-off from the new management team. To ensure engagement across the enterprise, roadshows were used to showcase what the data team was capable of delivering, combined with presentations to leadership groups, attendance at team meetings and webinars. As a consequence, the data office itself has created a new, engaged culture across the business which has embraced its potential – even the CEO has used the hashtag #dataisthenewoil in social media posts.

Fernqvist recalls: "I was asked to run what was the MI team at Zurich, and work with the team to determine a suitable data strategy for an organisation with a burning legacy landscape, high expectations and, in turn, frustrations.

"It did not start out big, or glamorous, but a strategy turned into a delivery roadmap, which in turn led to creating a data function, building a data asset, and developing a data culture across the organisation. We have since added predictive analytics and robotics, and now have a large function delivering on the second phase of the data and analytics strategy.

"We started small, battled to get our voices heard, and step-by-step built a mature data capability. There have been many successes, and just as many lessons learned the hard way. It has been quite a journey."

Identifying a gap between the vision which the organisation has for its operating model and the ability to deliver against it is a common experience. So, too, is launching the solution from within a constrained function which rapidly demonstrates value and evolves into a formal data office.

Samsung Europe is another example of a business that also in 2018 recognised the gap between its existing operations and the vision it had set for itself to "inspire the world, create the future" via richer digital experiences delivered through innovative technology and products. Internal processes and decision-making, however, were still rooted in legacy technologies. Although data-rich, much of this data existed in silos, meaning it took an average of 18 days for business intelligence (BI) teams to develop a data-driven insight. It also lacked any pan-European view of business performance across its 17 subsidiaries in over 34 countries.

To tackle this, the European consumer and market insights team adopted a new harmonised data model that allowed it to aggregate multiple data sets and present a consistent view to the business. This supports a weekly, country-level scorecard which is used by the European president of Samsung downwards to optimise media planning and spending, track sales and market share, and see how marketing is impacting on commercial Key Performance Indicators (KPIs).

But the real goal of this project was not to end up with a new BI tool, but rather to increase the level of data maturity and data literacy across the business, leading to evidence-based decision-making and a stronger focus on customer-centric activities. A user community of over 300 has been progressively increasing its ability to read, work with, analyse and argue with data in order to make recommendations for business activities across European markets.

Adopting a commercial vision for data

Setting a vision for the organisation has important consequences in terms of the business strategies that will be adopted, where value is expected to be created, the culture it operates and the enabling resources that are required. Success follows from approaching the task in this sequence, rather than looking at the existing resources that are in place and trying to wrap a new vision around them.

This concept of a sequential journey towards a high-performing business that has data in its DNA – a data literate organisation – is at the heart of the DataIQ Way. By focusing on the core dimensions and supporting pillars involved, rather than pursuing a single fix such as new data foundations, maturity can be progressively improved. This path is explained in detail in Chapter 3.

An example can be found at GSK Consumer Healthcare, the joint venture between GSK and Pfizer, which has the vision of becoming a stand-alone, world-leading provider of over-the-counter consumer healthcare products by 2022. To deliver against that goal, it has the stated strategy, "to focus on excellence in innovation to develop world-class brands, and on building our reputation through best-in-class interactions with retailers, healthcare professionals and shoppers".

To underpin all of this, a data office has been created from scratch which, during the course of 2020, grew from a headcount of four to a target of 50, overseen by GSK Consumer Healthcare's first global CDO, Wade Munsie. He has identified data literacy as a vital component, creating a common language and understanding around data across 94 global markets.

Crucially, the data office under his leadership is translating four elements of the company's vision into specific data activities. Munsie sets out the data vision as, "accelerating our human understanding, enabling bold decisions to fuel growth". This aligns the data strategy to the corporate vision across four pillars:

- *Trust* – building trust in data across the enterprise by getting the foundations right.

- *Empower* – unlocking the value of data to support and empower the business.

- *Beat the market* – using AI and data science to take analytics to the next level.

- *Mindset* – building a data-driven mindset across the enterprise.

Lloyd's of London, in another example of an organisation that has adopted a new vision, is pursuing a digital transformation and harnessing data to support these goals. Future at Lloyd's laid out the vision in a May 2019 prospectus, stating: "We are going to combine data, technology and new ways of working with our existing strengths to transform the culture we work in and everything we do – from placing risks and paying claims to attracting capital and developing new products."

Blueprint One was the ambitious plan for how it would progressively move towards this new target operating model. It included the goal that the business will be underpinned by "a data-first approach, evolving over time from a document world to a document-plus-data world to a data-first world". What Lloyd's has recognised is the potential for data to support this new vision if the right enabling resources are put in place. As the blueprint spelled out: "Data is not exciting by itself until it is defined, standardised and made available to the appropriate people; then, data is truly transformational to everything built on top of it." By the time an updated Blueprint Two was published in 2020, Lloyd's had recognised that data was the critical foundation on which its new digital operating model would be built.

Why data-driven is not a vision

Talk of data-fuelled industrial revolutions and market disruptions has created awareness of the potential of this resource right across the business world. In parallel with this recognition that a new vision might be possible there runs a level of anxiety. For one thing, it can seem to be too late to get in the game for companies that have not kicked off a digital transformation already or formalised their data strategy and assets. It can also seem like a domain reserved for global combines with turnovers running to billions of pounds, like GSK and Lloyd's of London, rather than an opportunity for companies at any scale.

One response to this can be a rush to adopt some form of data-driven activity in order to feel part of the trend. Typically, this might involve adopting data visualisation tools as part of a move away from Excel-based reporting, for example. BI is often a bridgehead for more complex data engineering and data integration.

What should not be assumed is that adopting new data tools is a vision in itself. Transformation does not happen because of tools and technology – it happens because the business has a vision of operating in a different way and achieving a different level of performance.

It is important to realise that, for all the advocacy around digital transformation and data as an asset, these are still early years. The technology aspects of this supposed revolution are easier to implement. According to research carried out by DataIQ in spring 2020, 41% of organisations claimed to be transforming the whole company to be digital-first. A further 42% had embarked on digital transformation within some of their departments. By contrast, the same study discovered that only 16% of organisations described their adoption and usage of data and analytics as advanced, with the majority (53%) saying they were still developing this capability.

Data-driven is not a vision in itself. But a vision that does not harness the transformational power of data is unlikely to succeed. A vision which embraces data as a core enabler moves closer to becoming reality by a critical step.

—————————— **DataIQ Way Marker** ——————————

Vision without data lacks perspective, data without vision lacks ambition

Structure

Data as a department

To achieve the vision of the organisation and execute on its business strategies, an organisational structure needs to be in place. This allows for tasks to be allocated, coordinated, supervised, measured and reported on. Many different organisational structures have been adopted to manage this, but in most cases specific functions exist to support common processes, such as sales, marketing, HR and IT. Specialised functions are efficient because they are able to deliver standardised, replicable approaches to recurring tasks.

Organisations have wrestled with the best way to assemble teams for nearly two centuries. Probably the first ever organisational chart was created in 1855. Called 'The New York & Erie Railroad diagram representing a plan of organisation exhibiting the division of administrative duties and showing the number and class of employés [sic] engaged in each department from the returns of September 1855', it is rightly hailed as a great early example of data visualisation, despite its complexity (see Figure 2.1 or visit https://tinyurl.com/y5fv6y2c). As can be seen clearly, this is a very linear organisation based around geography and product lines, with few of the overarching functions that a modern organisation would expect to see.

Figure 2.1: New York and Erie Railroad

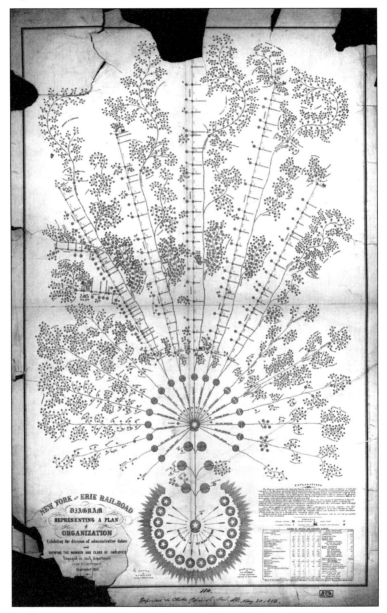

Source: Library of Congress, Geography and Map Division

This operational and manufacturing-led view of organisations and their functions continued until the 1930s when recognising the role of overarching functions, such as sales and marketing, led to their establishment. These then continued relatively unchanged until the 1980s, which saw a number of significant transformations, such as that of accounting into finance as company flotations and market listings demanded more focus on asset and revenue management, while the recognition of people as a critical business asset from the 1990s onwards saw personnel departments rebranded as human resources. Nowadays, these functions are common in all organisations and well understood to be essential.

Data as a department is a much more recent phenomenon, requiring the emergence of data from within the IT function as a specific area of focus in the twenty-first century. Two trends have driven this:

- The first is the accelerating adoption of digital technology, initiated by the commercialisation of the internet in the late 1990s.

- The second is growing regulation of data as a specific area of concern, not just within data protection legislation – such as the EU's GDPR, California's Consumer Privacy Act or the UK's DPA – but also within industry-specific legislation, especially financial services and regulations such as Know Your Customer and Anti-Money Laundering, which have profound data implications.

Recognising this, organisations have progressively been turning to the data office as a specific department to own the issue of data governance (including data protection, privacy and data quality) and increasingly value creation through data analytics. This has been a relatively slow-growing trend, however. Capital One appointed probably the first CDO in 2002, while Yahoo! made a more high-profile appointment in 2005, but overall numbers remained low until about 2008–2010 when the post-financial crisis response of banks included introducing the CDO role and the creation of data as a department. Many had been scared into this by the recognition that they did not know as a reconciled number how many net customers they had, what balances or debts they held and therefore what their total exposure was likely to be.

While logical, creating a data office and recognising that data needs a stand-alone department is complicated. This is because of the horizontal nature of data as an activity across any organisation – it is fed by and supports virtually every other function in some way, rather than being a vertical function in its own right. In many respects, it can look exactly like the New York & Erie Railroad chart in Figure 2.1 with nodes and spurs feeding from every part of the business. For this reason, data is often incubated (and constrained) within an existing function, such as marketing or finance, while it begins the task of establishing standards, common data models and integration of data sets, and then feeds back reports, insights and data products to the business.

Research carried out by DataIQ in 2020 revealed that these internal business processes and operations were as likely to be the focus of the data office as more external customer-facing activities. When asked about their business purpose for collecting personal data, out of the top four reasons given, two were customer-oriented – optimising the customer journey (80.6%) and tailoring content to each individual (61.2%) – while two were entirely business process-oriented – fuelling analytics (73.5%) and measuring business performance (69.4%).

This demonstrates both the breadth of tasks in which the data office may find itself involved and also the key role data now plays in driving the business and its decision-making.

———————— DataIQ Way Marker ————————

Recognise data formally in your organisation
and build from there

▼

Aligning data with the business

With the recognition that data requires specific status as a department comes the need to decide where it will sit within the organisation. As has already been noted, the horizontal nature of data's role makes it a difficult piece to fit into any organisational chart. But as EY wrote in a 2018 report, *Becoming an analytics-driven organisation to create value*, putting data into the organisational chart – rather than allowing it to exist either in multiple places or to operate without formal recognition – affects the level of impact it can have.

"Without the right organisational structures, processes and governance frameworks in place, it is impossible to collect and analyse data from across the enterprise and deliver insight where it is most needed. This results in a siloed approach to big data deployment that limits a company's ability to find, measure, create and protect value across diverse operational areas," wrote the authors.

It is a reflection of the recency of the concept of data as a department and its low level of maturity that there are no consistent models for what the correct organisational structure should look like. As a result, different businesses address the issue in a wide variety of ways and the last five years have been typified by regular restructuring of CDO reporting lines:

- easyJet replaced its chief customer officer with a CDO in April 2018 reporting to the CEO, then in May 2019 created the new, combined role of chief data and information officer leading a new data function to support its vision of becoming the world's leading data-driven airline.

- Sainsbury's hired a new group chief information officer (CIO) in 2018 to handle the grocery chain, Sainsbury's bank, Argos and then newly acquired Nectar division. The incoming CIO laid claim to the data and analytics office which had been created the previous year.

- Royal Mail established its data office as an independent function, then in early 2017 moved it to sit under one of three CIOs who report to the chief customer officer. But it also created a stand-alone function of advanced analytics, leaving the governance responsibilities with the CDO.

- GSK Consumer Healthcare established its data office in late 2019, initially reporting to the chief digital officer, but that role was subsequently eliminated and a new reporting line to the CIO put in place.

DataIQ research and discussions by this author with data leaders reveal that most are less concerned about where they sit in the organisation and what their line of reporting will be than with their level of top-down support and ability to influence business stakeholders. One thing is clear, however. Placing data within the IT function (for example, as a direct report to the CIO) is a mistake as it typically constrains both the breadth of data's domain and also its sphere of influence. Data is most effective when it is either an independent department with a reporting line into the board, or has a value-creating department as its host.

—————————— **DataIQ Way Marker** ——————————

The voice of data needs to be heard in the boardroom – not just in the back room

▼

Upsides and downsides of structures

The purpose of creating any type of department is to allow tasks to be allocated, coordinated, supervised, measured and reported on. Given the range of sources from which data is derived and the breadth of processes it then supports, the argument for creating a data office in some form is difficult to withstand.

Formalising data into a department also addresses some of the critical aspects of data as an asset:

- *Standards* – establishing common standards (such as data definitions, data models, data quality, data governance) and shared ways of working.

- *Collaborative development* – developing data projects and analytics briefs in close cooperation across functional teams, especially where offshore or external business partners are involved.

- *Knowledge sharing* – creating visibility across all practitioners of the work stack as well as the tools and techniques available.

- *Connections* – ensuring data and analytics practitioners feel part of a community of practice.

Data and analytics undoubtedly benefit from the 'network effect' where the value of the service increases with the number of people using/delivering it. For a majority of organisations, the solution to the challenges above is to create a centralised data or analytics centre of excellence (ACE or DACE) where all practitioners are co-located, or combined into a small number of grouped operations.

Yet this is not necessarily appropriate or achievable for all organisations for a number of reasons. A prime argument against centralisation is where it is more effective to adopt a federated approach in which analysts are embedded alongside their business stakeholders, either individually or as teams (and even whole functions in some cases).

Having analysts embedded in the business is critical to how effective their outputs are and how well-aligned they are to business needs. At one mobile network operator, 60% of analysts were embedded, taking part in line of business meetings as well as having their own team meetings. Their presence alongside stakeholders helps because it means they adopt the same ways of working.

The downside of a non-centralised data function, whether federated or hub-and-spoke, is that it usually requires more management effort (and a degree of political skill) to maintain effectiveness and motivation. Meeting schedules can become congested where practitioners are also engaging with their stakeholder function, for example, while specific resources, such as digital platforms, may be blocked by the governance rules in regulated industries.

Perhaps as a result of this, as Table 2.1 shows, data capabilities are 50% more likely to operate from a centralised department as they are to be federated into lines of business. The implications for where tasks get carried out are considered in more detail below.

Table 2.1: Data offices within the organisation

	(%)
Centralised or centre of excellence	43.2
Distributed or federated	27.0
Hub-and-spoke	13.5
Consulting	13.5
Other	2.7

Roles

Translating tasks into roles

Data and analytics tasks can be assigned to roles in a wide variety of ways, including by historical role definitions, specific skills, resource availability, urgency and so forth. The location of these roles may be influenced by the desired operating model as outlined earlier (centralised, federated, etc.), but equally may reflect the level of data dependency of stakeholders.

An incubating function, such as marketing or finance, may absorb a wide range of roles, often in parallel with each other. Having multiple roles undertaking similar tasks is not necessarily inefficient – it can be a requirement of different roles to undertake overlapping tasks (i.e. reporting, data visualisation, data preparation).

Typically, tasks will cluster within roles and roles will also cluster within functions according to the depth of data and analytics dependency they have (see Figure 2.2). Centralisation of tasks into a data and analytics centre of excellence, for example, may be more efficient as it allows for an activity to be undertaken once and shared multiple times.

Federated data organisations can achieve a similar efficiency while remaining close to their internal customers, provided there is good visibility and communication between these practitioners and a recognition of their role in serving multiple internal customers, not just the function in which they are based.

Figure 2.2: Clustering of tasks within roles and functions

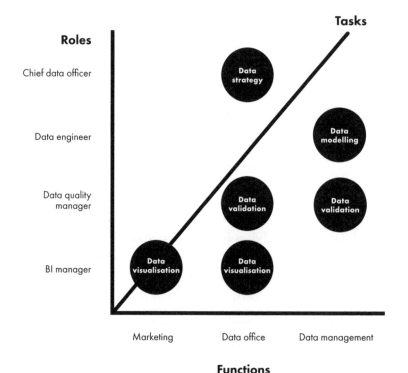

To federate or to centralise?

In a traditional organisational structure, roles are created according to the needs/demands of each function, rather than as a reflection of the task resourcing required. For example, each business function might create its own BI manager role in order to remove that task from other roles.

The closer to the point of use that a task sits, the more likely it is to have a role created for it (e.g. marketing will often have its own database manager), while tasks that sit further away from a business process often do not have a specific role created for them (e.g. data governance).

As a consequence, task duplication is almost inevitable within a conventional organisation (see Table 2.2), while task neglect is typical because of a lack of function ownership.

Table 2.2: Data tasks within conventional organisations

Task	Role	Function
Data validation	Data quality manager	Data management, Marketing
Privacy policy definition	In-house counsel, data protection officer	Legal, compliance, DPO office
Data mastering	MDM manager	Data management, Line of business
Metadata management	None	None

Role duplication is an extension of task duplication within conventional organisational structures. This is because functions create roles to deliver the data tasks they require close to the point of use (see Table 2.3). The issue with function-level role creation is that best practice does not get shared, knowledge transfer is limited and gaps in provisioning go unnoticed. It can also lead to competing views on key numbers, such as net customer base or demand forecasts.

Table 2.3: Data roles within conventional organisational structures

Function	Role	Task
Analytics	Customer churn analyst	Churn propensity modelling
Customer management	Retention manager	Churn propensity modelling
Marketing	Customer marketing manager	Churn propensity modelling
Board	Chief customer officer	Creating single view of the customer
Data management	Customer database manager	Creating single view of the customer
Business intelligence	Customer analyst	Net customer figure report
Finance	Chief financial officer	Net customer figure report
Compliance	KYC manager	Identity validation
Ecommerce	Channel manager	Identity validation
Information security	Information security officer	Identity validation
Customer experience	Cx manager	Behavioural modelling
Data science	Data scientist	Behavioural modelling

Centralisations of roles, for example into a data and analytics centre of excellence, removes role and task duplication while supporting multiple internal customers (see Table 2.4). A similar multi-stakeholder effect can be achieved by using a virtual data and analytics organisation where roles are based within a specific business function, but serve multiple stakeholders across functions.

Management of this virtual data and analytics organisation can be more challenging due to the pressures and immediacy of the host function's deadlines compared to stakeholders elsewhere in the organisation. Service level agreements are important, as is political cover and protection for these roles when conflicts arise between competing deadlines.

Table 2.4: Data roles within a centre of excellence: task-based view of customer data roles

Task	Role	Function	Customers
Creating single view of the customer	Customer database manager	Data and analytics centre of excellence	Marketing
Net customer figure report	Customer analyst	Data and analytics centre of excellence	Board, Marketing
Churn propensity modelling	Customer churn analyst	Data and analytics centre of excellence	Marketing
Behavioural modelling	Data scientist	Data and analytics centre of excellence	Cx management
Identity validation	Information security officer	Information security	Ecommerce

The reality of multi-stakeholder data and analytics tasks

Data and analytics tasks are rarely unique to a single function since the way in which data or models are defined, distributed and operationalised inevitably involves multiple roles. Unless these have been centralised, these roles will sit within multiple functions, so any data-driven process involves a level of project management.

This project management, without the leadership of a centralised data and analytics department or a virtual organisation, can be one of the most challenging aspects of achieving these tasks. This is particularly true of tasks which are not owned by any one function (e.g. data governance).

Tasks can be categorised in such a way that the process required to ensure they are achieved becomes visible. Example categories are:

- communication

- definition

- distribution

- monitoring

- reporting

- operationalisation

- ongoing management

- remediation

- training.

Not every task will involve every category, while some will involve all (and potentially additional) categories. An example of how tasks can be categorised and their multi-stakeholder nature identified is given in Table 2.5 for data quality.

Table 2.5: Categorising tasks and assigning to functions (conventional organisation)

Definition	Distribution	Monitoring/ Control	Reporting	Operationalisation	Ongoing management	Remediation	Communication	Training
Task: Data collection policy	Task: Data collection processes	Task: Data collection	Task: Data KPIs	Task: Data collection	Task: Data storage	Task: Data correction	Task: Policy changes	Task: Policy adherence
Function: Data strategy	Function: Data management	Function: Ecommerce, Marketing	Function: Data management	Function: IT	Function: IT, Data management	Function: Data quality, Data management	Function: Data management, Marketing	Function: Data management
Task: Data standard		Task: Metadata control		Task: Data steward	Task: Database software maintenance	Task: Metadata correction	Task: Data steward recruitment	
Function: Data management		Function: Data quality, Data management		Function: Ecommerce, Marketing, Sales, CRM	Function: IT, Data management	Function: Data quality, Data management	Function: Data strategy	

Establishment and headcount

While assigning tasks to roles is a relatively straightforward issue, deciding how many of each role is required within the organisation is less simple to define. This is often because there is low visibility of the volume of demand for each task to support a definition of establishment levels across the headcount. Understanding the value of these tasks is even more challenging. For example, if multiple functions need to create specific reports on KPIs, this could lead to an excessive headcount of BI roles unless a review is carried out of those reports, leading to optimisation and even retiring of many unused metrics.

When creating a data office from scratch, one of the first tasks is often to undertake exactly this type of review, taking ownership of KPI reporting and reducing the workload to a manageable level. If this is not done, the data office will not be able to move from being reactive – delivering against stakeholder demands as and when they arise – to being proactive – leading stakeholders with insights derived from standardised data.

One of the main arguments for adopting a task-based view of roles is cost-effectiveness. The market for data practitioners is overheated at almost all levels, leading to salary inflation, which is exaggerated within certain in-demand roles, such as data science or data engineering. If these are broken down into task sets, it may be possible to define a role that does not have the inflationary role name but still delivers the right skills and abilities.

───────────── **DataIQ Way Marker** ─────────────

Getting tasks done is more important than what
you call the person doing them

▼

DATA LITERACY STEPCOUNTER

Data literacy has to be an enterprise-wide endeavour which sees data as indispensable to achieving corporate goals.

The data department has to establish and manage itself effectively to support this.

Steps 4–6:

4. Translate the corporate vision into a data vision and keep them closely aligned.

5. Establish a data office, ideally as an independent department with direct reporting to the board.

6. Define roles within the data department by the tasks required to avoid duplication of effort.

CHAPTER 3
Becoming data literate

Roadmap – in this chapter:

- Aviva changed its culture to be customer-centric using data science.

- Data literacy has five dimensions: vision, business strategy, value creation, culture and data foundations.

- Each of these needs the support of four pillars: strategy, leadership, skills and enablers.

- Maturity can be measured against these dimensions and pillars and mapped into five stages: data user, data-driven, data literate, data cultured, data native.

Aviva builds a customer-centric culture

H OW DO YOU transform a legacy organisation so that it is able to unlock new value and put a fresh proposition in front of customers who risk being lost to digital disruptors? Aviva started on this journey in 2016 with the creation of its customer science team as part of a vision to create engaging, relevant customer experiences through intelligent use of data science. A key moment occurred in 2019 when this team realised it needed to make customer data central and relevant to the whole organisation. This would enable data science to avoid being just another siloed department by bringing data science to life for colleagues and providing a common language for the business to talk about customers.

Of course, data foundations were important. In this example, a unified customer view brought together over 70 databases from multiple business units. This integrated data set holds more than 15bn data points on 16m customers covering product holding, demographics and behavioural indicators – the largest customer data set in UK insurance.

But as Tom Spencer, head of customer data science at Aviva, notes, the data asset in itself would not lead to customer-centricity. "Essential to the success of this work was close collaboration with partner colleagues across the organisation, including a customer accelerator team. Our steering group had representatives from the different business units in order to make sure that from the start, this was a journey that we were taking the whole business on together," he said.

At the level of business strategy, the company wanted to move forward from conventional age- and affluence-based rules models by developing a new data science-led customer segmentation using machine learning (ML). Crucially, says Spencer, "in order to achieve cultural change, the segmentation had to be simple and to bring our customers to life for our colleagues."

This saw a top level of seven customer clusters defined, underpinned by micro-level segments to support a wide range of use and business cases. These were made available via a microsite and also embedded into a reporting layer which now sees regular MI reports created based around the clusters.

Communication went further to drive adoption across the organisation. "We worked with front-line call centre colleagues to give each of the seven segments a memorable name and signature colour, present on all the segmentation collateral at the different worksites. We then identified 100 customers who were representative of each segment and filmed interviews with them to bring the customers to life. These videos and imagery then were presented in collaboration with 150 'super users' across five sites as part of the rollout," says Spencer.

"The segmentation's power is in making our customers come alive for colleagues and allowing all of them to access cutting-edge machine learning. This transforms Aviva's ability to drive better customer outcomes and business results with a data-led approach.

"In our industry, the challenge is not about appreciating the value of data per se. Data is, and always has been, central to insurance companies. Rather, the challenge lies in understanding that the sources and applications of data have massively evolved, and then ensuring that organisational structures, strategies, business models and ways of working keep pace."

As this example demonstrates, there is more to consider when driving data literacy than just the data foundations. Aviva recognised that the company vision needed to be translated into a business strategy which would lead to value creation. With the right data enablers, this made it possible to start changing the culture of the business.

These five dimensions – vision, business strategy, value creation, culture, data foundations – are at the heart of the DataIQ Way, as the next section outlines. By addressing each of them, an organisation can gradually increase its level of maturity around data and analytics and find the path to becoming data literate and beyond.

Five dimensions of the DataIQ Way

───────── **DataIQ Way Marker** ─────────

Data drives value, value delivers the vision

▼

Becoming data literate and increasing the maturity of data and analytics adoption involves specific actions and constant effort. For data leaders, part of the mission has to be pursuing this goal and being the change agent. As we have seen in previous chapters, the CDO is often tasked initially with putting in place core data foundations. Ensuring this is not the limit of the role is essential – we will explore this further in Chapter 6.

The DataIQ Way has been developed to support and guide data leaders and CDOs on this journey with clear staging points and steps to count. Based on our extensive evidence base, we have identified the common elements of successful data transformations. Across these, five dimensions stand out as being central to programmes that build a new culture based on data:

- Vision

- Business strategy

- Value creation

- Culture
- Data foundations.

First dimension: Vision

Every organisation needs a vision. This declaration of purpose ensures that every activity and decision is aligned to clear goals or will support progress towards the ultimately desired state.

Each organisation will have its own vision – it may be to disrupt a market or deliver innovative services; it may be to protect investors' wealth or to support vulnerable individuals. Often, there will be a legacy of purpose that needs to be redefined for changed circumstances, but which draws on a consistent set of values or principles.

One of those changed circumstances is the ability to adopt data and apply it to the way the organisation operates. But becoming data-driven is not a vision in its own right – it is typical of enterprises that are at lower levels of maturity that they have an existing vision to which data and analytics are retro-fitted, or that the goal is to enable access to data across the organisation.

Laudable and necessary as these approaches are, they still treat data as external to the vision, rather than as part of the operational DNA. A truly visionary organisation sets out its vision with an inherent assumption that data and analytics will be deployed against its goals, just as other departments – sales, finance, HR, IT – are assumed to be involved.

Second dimension: Business strategy

In order to realise the vision, the organisation has to decide what actions it will take in pursuing these goals. That might mean pursuing acquisitions to fuel growth or partnering with others to deliver a new ecosystem of services.

Typically, the business strategy is set with a horizon of three to five years, with annual updates to reflect milestones achieved or missed. Key business functions are represented on the strategy board, but historically this has not included data (not least because a central data office may not have existed before).

As the organisation matures in its use of data and analytics, it will move from referencing data within its strategy through alignment of the data strategy with the business strategy to the point where data is an equal stakeholder in the process and its role is innate to the various actions agreed upon. This will require a data leader with the political skills to represent the department at the most senior level.

Third dimension: Value creation

Alignment between the business strategy and the organisational vision should be total in order to avoid dilution of effort through the pursuit of non-core objectives. Similarly, the business strategy should be built on value-creating activities, otherwise the horizon line for success will continually be pushed further out.

For data and analytics, the ideal is to achieve direct association between its engagement with the business and the value being created. An ultimate outcome of this could be the inclusion of data as an asset on the corporate balance sheet, although current accounting practices do not properly support this.

En route, it is essential for business stakeholders to recognise value creation that is attributable to data and analytics so these departments can avoid being purely a cost centre. Formal value recognition within processes and projects is achievable, but not yet common. Until this is in place, recognising a proportion of incremental gains or cost reductions through informal agreements or proxy measures can begin to establish a culture of value creation being linked to data.

Forth dimension: Culture

The culture of an organisation is created in a variety of different ways, some formal, many informal. Ideally, the visible, written culture explains how employees are expected to behave, the values they should seek to represent and how performance is measured and rewarded. A healthy, thriving culture makes the task of management easier because specific actions do not need to be directed as they will be initiated organically. Some cultures are generic, such as the concept of the start-up culture, while others need more effort and support to become embedded.

Data is a newcomer to the world of organisational culture and often deliberately sets up with a different approach from the main enterprise. This can be powerful when data needs to act as a change agent, but it can also lead to conflict – other departments may express frustration that they are not given the same level of freedom, for example.

In an organisation at the highest level of maturity in its adoption of data and analytics, there will be a clear voice for this department at board-level or even across all roles at the table. Building towards this state will see data increasingly integrated into lines of business or federated across stakeholder departments, closing any gaps between the data culture and company culture through shared objectives, metrics and rewards.

Fifth dimension: Data foundations

Along the pathway to full maturity, a range of enabling data and technology will be required, from foundational data assets (such as new generation data platforms and data integration) to advanced solutions (such as robotic process automation and AI). Each of these is capable of yielding competitive advantage or value, through driving incremental revenue or achieving cost savings.

It is important to recognise the role that these solutions play in supporting progression towards the vision, but equally to understand that they do not deliver it in their own right. Without key data foundations, the business strategy will not succeed and the vision will remain unrealised. With these enablers in place, strategies can be pursued to their desired outcome.

Choosing which of the enabling data and technologies to adopt at each stage is one of the critical success factors of any transformation. Few organisations have the resources or appetite to adopt all options at once – a phased roadmap is essential, as well as sufficient flexibility to respond to changing circumstances.

Four pillars of the DataIQ Way

To make progress towards the desired state of data literacy, you need to put in place each of the five dimensions outlined above. Your method for doing this should be based around four pillars. Each of these has been seen by DataIQ to create the right conditions for advancing the organisational capabilities, intelligence and outcomes from data.

The four pillars are:

- *Strategy* – defining exactly how you intend to pursue the goal of the project.

- *Leadership* – showing the direction of travel and encouraging everybody involved to follow the path.

- *Skills* – recognising the breadth of abilities that are required within each dimension, from core competencies to soft skills.

- *Enablers* – choosing the right solutions and business partners to support the project.

─────────────── **DataIQ Way Marker** ───────────────

You don't only need a map, you need to know how to read it

▼

Pillar 1 – Strategy

For vision – creating a vision for the organisation sets the horizon line for what it wants to achieve. Reaching that ideal end state may never happen – along the way, changes to market conditions, ownership, structure and much more will reorient the business and even reset the vision. A critical skill for the data leader is to ensure data remains central to the purpose being pursued.

For business strategy – as the business strategy evolves in line with shifting circumstances, data needs to have a rolling strategy to remain at the leading edge and to ensure its relevance to a progressive organisation. Strategic initiatives like AI and ML will rapidly become mainstream – constant market scanning for emerging opportunities or disruptors should be written into the data strategy.

For value creation – one key to maintaining relevance and impact is to identify specific financial measures of the value being created by data and analytics. This should be considered at a strategic level, such as delivery to the bottom line, supporting the share price, enhancing productivity or other fundamental business metrics, as well as within the context of specific projects and activities.

For culture – when advancing the culture of the organisation, the data office needs a strategy for how to embed the right behaviours within the leadership teams and their departments. Some aspects of culture are easier to develop, such as customer-facing ones, than internal activities which may have deeply rooted ways of working that can be hard to change. A strategy of cultural transformation needs to run alongside process transformations to address this.

For data foundations – with data written into the organisation's DNA as one of the five dimensions, everything becomes based on it and feeds into and off it. All technology and digital strategies need to embrace this and be informed by what has already been created on the back of the data strategy. It also needs to evolve in line with emerging technologies.

Pillar 2 – Leadership

For vision – becoming data literate will involve changes to the senior leadership of the business and therefore the leadership required within the data office. As board members increasingly possess a high level of data literacy and cognisance of what is possible, the distinction between the CDO and the C-suite will dissolve. A new vision will be necessary for what the CDO brings to the table.

For business strategy – test-and-learn will become part of the working method across the enterprise, not just within data science and analytics. There will be no fear of failure, but rather a desire to fail fast in order to identify successful strategies. Ensuring engagement by the board with external innovators, especially those outside of the sector or domain, should be part of the leadership provided by the CDO.

For value creation – if the data office has tied its actions to bottom-line impacts, the CDO will need to step up as a business leader, taking ownership and responsibility for value creation at the deepest level. Tying personal financial rewards to these numbers is the last link in the chain which keeps value creation and vision on all sides of the business close to each other.

For culture – numbers are not the only pillar that needs strong leadership – part of becoming data literate will involve performance measurement that tracks use of data against outcomes, including the hit rate of decision-makers and the accuracy of models. Closing this loop between using data to make decisions and identifying when the outcomes fall within the expected parameters should be part of a continuous improvement culture.

For data foundations – the CDO will also need to keep their understanding of what other functions are trying to achieve up to date in order to align with those objectives and future-proof their own projects.

Pillar 3 – Skills

For vision – if data skills become deeply embedded in the organisation from top to bottom, the data literate organisation will be a clear leader in its sector and practices. It should ensure focus is kept on attracting the candidates with the best skills at all levels during recruitment. As part of its vision, there should be a forward-looking idea of what new data and analytics abilities need to be brought onboard.

For business strategy – a data skills strategy should include the use of automation on activities that are time-consuming, but relatively low value, to replace the need for basic skills.

For value creation – for the CDO, developing business skills and financial acumen are likely to be critical in order to remain at the top table. At the same time, predictive analytics are likely to be further embedded into the CFO's role and this department may become the leading stakeholder in data.

For culture – upshifting access and usage from entry-level tools to sophisticated self-service is challenging, not least because of the difficulties of balancing analytics and governance. Organisations that are born digital are more likely to have the skills in place to make this work – legacy organisations need to focus on creating highly-skilled practitioners across the board.

For data foundations – career-long learning and support will also be needed to keep the skillset of the data offices relevant. And even highly data literate organisations can struggle to learn the fundamental lessons from their successes, rather than banking them and moving forward. Building in both time and procedures to capture these insights can ensure knowledge is retained and leveraged.

Pillar 4 – Enablers

For vision – advanced data and analytics are enablers of the vision for the organisation, but saturation point may be reached in terms of internal capabilities. Finding external partners and start-ups who can introduce a new generation of tools and techniques will keep the pace of innovation high.

For business strategy – agile working should be used at every level, including the development of the data strategy and business strategy, to ensure the organisation remains flexible and able to adapt rapidly. As part of the overarching business strategy, the organisation should continually identify working practices that are relevant and enabling for its goals, adapting as necessary and discarding practices that have outlived their usefulness.

For value creation – formal, accountancy-grade metrics for the impact of data are a high-level enabler of data's influence and impact. The missing link is to an accounting standard for data that is acceptable to the data industry – engagement between the two parties needs to take place with a strong focus on how to measure value creation, not just as a low-grade intangible asset.

For culture – removing barriers to the access and adoption of data and technology will keep the culture aligned across the organisation, thereby avoiding a two-speed enterprise in which the benefits and value from these tools is primarily gained by a small group.

For data foundations – since data is fundamental to the business model of a highly data literate organisation, it goes without saying that appropriate budget and authority need to be in place for the CDO. While no budget line is ever immune to scrutiny and challenge, the impact on the business of any scaling back or resizing needs to be made evident as part of any assessment.

The DataIQ Way Maturity Box

Five levels of maturity

The five dimensions that drive data literacy combined with the four pillars that support each of them can be combined in a 5 × 4 matrix against which progress can be mapped and assessed using tools like DataIQ CARBON™.

Using the insight gained from these assessments, the DataIQ Way has identified five levels of maturity that reflect what has been achieved across these 20 aspects. As shown in Table 3.1, these are:

Data user – an organisation that is primarily using data in an ad hoc fashion with few repeatable processes or alignment to strategic goals.

Data-driven – an organisation that is building processes using data and has initiated formal structures as a way of gaining a competitive advantage.

Data literate – an organisation in which data has been made accessible and evidence-based decision-making is beginning to be practised.

Data cultured – an organisation which has data embedded across the enterprise and where strategic development is informed by data.

Data native – an organisation where there is no distinction between data and the business.

Progress is likely to be differential on each dimension and pillar depending on the level when this framework is adopted, but ultimately, it is possible to bring the business close to the ideal of being data native.

Table 3.1: The DataIQ Way maturity box

	Vision	Business strategy	Value creation	Culture	Enablers
Data native	Our organisation's vision is fully informed and supported by data	There is no distinction between our business strategy and data strategy – they are fully integrated	We have formal recognition of the value created from data to metrics accepted by the CFO	Data has board-level representation	We continuously improve our data capability and transfer best practices as part of knowledge sharing
Data cultured	Our organisation's vision sees data as a competitive advantage	Our business strategy and data strategy are developed in unison	We have formal recognition of value from data accepted by each stakeholder	Our CDO is recognised as a peer by business leaders	We have provisioned data tools across the business, with central governance
Data literate	Our organisation's vision includes data democratisation	Our business strategy aligns with our data strategy, although they are developed separately	We acknowledge a proportion of revenue/ cost savings etc. as deriving from data	We have established a central data office	We have enabled self-service reporting
Data-driven	Our organisation's vision implies adoption of data as an ongoing intention	Our business strategy includes increasing the maturity of our data usage	We have identified data as an opportunity to create incremental gains	Our data teams respond to requests ad hoc	We have integrated most customer data, but not all
Data user	Our organisation's vision is created as a stand-alone	Our business strategy does not reference data and analytics	We find the data required as a point solution for predetermined projects	We have limited engagement between data and the business	We have multiple data sources that are not integrated with no overall governance

Data literacy and the data literate organisation

Defining data literacy

In following the DataIQ Way and addressing the foundations and dimensions it includes, the goal should be to reach a sustainable, steady state for the organisation. Becoming data literate is a realistic goal which can be achieved within a two- to three-year time frame, either as a specific, stand-alone project or within the context of a broader business transformation, such as becoming digital-first.

An organisation that is data literate must be confident that these five core statements would be affirmed across the organisation by senior leaders, business stakeholders and the data department itself:

1. *We know the value of data* – data is part of our vision; data aligns with our business strategy; data creates value; data provides evidence and insight for decisions.

2. *We have the data we need* – our data strategy enables our business processes; we have mastered and governed our data asset; we have a thriving data ecosystem.

3. *We use the data we have* – we use evidence-based decision-making; we have enabled the business with self-service data access and reporting; we have created replicable data products.

4. *We trust the data we have* – the data we use is fully compliant, secure and governed; our data stands up to scrutiny by the business; our data office is a trusted and credible guardian.

5. *We share a common data culture* – data is part of our ways of working; data skills are supported, developed and valued; we communicate about data using a shared language.

Typically, the ability to say yes to each of these will be differential between the statements and even between departments. Using the data which the organisation holds is often the easiest since data foundations are where data offices and CDOs enter the picture. Sharing a common data culture is much harder, but this can develop out of those same data initiatives. Carlo Nebuloni, transformation director and CDO at AXA UK and Ireland, puts it this way: "Always use concrete examples to demonstrate the power of data. Never just give the logical, technical argument – make it real, i.e. 'implementing a data dictionary will reduce the initial phase of the next use case from six weeks to less than one week'."

There is also a risk in assuming that once the state of data literacy has been achieved, the organisation will remain at that level or even progress. But real-world experience shows that constant disruption can have a negative impact – as much as the organisation is pushing ahead with data-driven projects, other strategic goals might interfere by taking away attention, resources or political support.

For this reason, an initial assessment which is repeated after a specific period of time (typically one year or at the conclusion of a data literacy programme) is a valuable tool in measuring whether this state has been achieved and maintained. Similarly, data literacy programmes need to be refreshed and reinforced to ensure alignment and also support progress towards a higher state of data culture.

How do we score our data literacy?

For an organisation to claim to be genuinely data literate, it needs to consider two facets of the same coin:

- "Outside in" – to what extent are the consumers of data within the business – the stakeholders for the data department – able to understand data and bring it to bear in their thinking and decision-making?

- "Inside out" – to what extent are the producers of data – primarily the data department itself – aligned with the needs and goals of the business?

Looking at the issue in this way moves the conversation on from simple technical skills (e.g. coding, reporting, data visualisation) and numeracy (e.g. understanding statistics) and into the critical realms of mindset and behaviour (see Figure 3.1). For business stakeholders, this ranges from having a conversational ability in the language of data (supported by data foundations like a data dictionary, for example) through to data interpretation and evidence-based decision-making. For data practitioners, teams and leaders, this creates two hand-off points – data foundations, which have been curated by individuals who are fluent in the language of data, and data translation, which sees the outputs from analytics being expressed in terms the whole business shares without the obstacles of technical vocabulary or misaligned concepts.

Surveying both sides, either through extensive self-assessment or by canvassing the views of critical parties such as the CDO and business leaders, will indicate whether data literacy has been achieved. Typically, such a process will identify areas in which the level meets or even exceeds the current need, but also gaps that must be addressed.

Figure 3.1: The building blocks of the data literate organisation

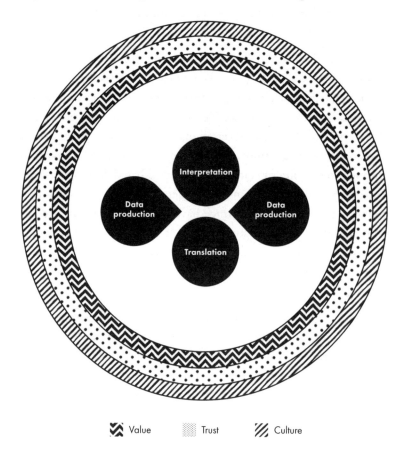

Why data-driven does not equal data literate

While there has been an accelerated interest in data as a transformational resource, the growing maturity of its adoption has not necessarily converted into data literacy. As Figure 3.2 shows, there is a definite lag between the introduction of a data department (including the provisioning of access and analytical insights) and the creation of a data literate business, as DataIQ research revealed.

While four out of ten organisations rate their level of data maturity as either Advanced or Reaching maturity, only 25% say their company either has widely democratised data (3.4%) or are at an advanced state in many areas of the business (21.4%). With six in ten describing data skills generally as only moderate, that leaves a significant gap in understanding into which projects could fall and where the risk of failure increases.

Figure 3.2: Adoption of data and level of data literacy

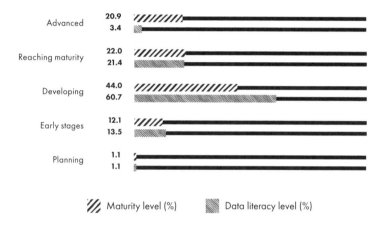

DATA LITERACY STEPCOUNTER

Becoming data literate has to be an active strategy for the organisation with support and buy-in across the enterprise.

Data literacy needs to be monitored and sustained once achieved.

Steps 7–9:

7. Take the full spectrum view of how data will drive your organisation across its vision, business strategy, value creation, culture and data foundations.

8. Focus on supporting each of these with a strategy, leadership, skills and enablers.

9. Constantly push to increase the level of maturity around data and becoming data literate (and beyond).

CHAPTER 4
Business strategy and data strategy

Roadmap – in this chapter:

- Jaguar Land Rover used a collaborative approach to developing management information to drive behavioural change.

- Aligning the data strategy with the business strategy is central to improving data literacy.

- Investment use cases fall into four categories: technology, headcount, toolkits, innovation.

- Use cases have a higher success rate if they focus on business challenges.

- As data skills become more embedded in business, the nature of work and the future of jobs will evolve.

- Skills assessment and mapping will identify the true capability of the data department but needs to be future-focused too.

- Engaging stakeholders effectively happens through four habits: collaborating, communicating, championing, challenging.

- The data leader should ensure a close fit between the data strategy and the business strategy.

Adopt

Jaguar Land Rover drives data adoption with MI

IN 2018, JAGUAR Land Rover brought together marketing, sales, service and regional operations into a quartet led by the chief commercial officer (COO). Facing significant business and market challenges, such as hostility towards diesel engines and the UK's decision on Brexit, the COO wanted full spectrum insight into commercial performance across all major global markets. However, there was no integrated source for this data that had been curated from the multiple legacy data systems and architectures across the organisation.

The decision was taken to commission a new management information system (MIS) to be led by the newly formed commercial and customer analytics team. Although seed budget and resourcing was in place, the team was small and realised that cultural and operational issues would be a bigger challenge than data and technology.

It would need to win the trust and cooperation of stakeholders, ensuring they would support the global ambition while feeling their local needs and conventions would still be respected. The MIS needed to achieve maximum coverage across silos, requiring buy-in from regional CEOs, but with minimal disruption.

To achieve this, the team adopted five people-focused principles for its stakeholder engagement:

Principle 1 – Collaboration

The team drew on its relationships and network within the new commercial unit to co-create the plan for the MIS. This was important in order to avoid it being perceived as a one-off project instead of strategic initiative. By tuning into local sensitivities, such as language, culture and differing attitudes towards numbers across markets, it ensured the project was not perceived as an ivory tower, top-down programme. This extended to establishing a proactive and mutually challenging relationship with IT which provisioned key tools.

Principle 2 – Crowdsourcing

Timely and accurate reporting was developed as a collective effort with ownership and responsibility shared among stakeholders. This involved entrepreneurial negotiation with stakeholders that yielded reporting at scale and depth. The MIS now processes 226bn data points each day yielded from 75 sources to create 550 metrics.

Principle 3 – Flexibility

Agile, sprint-based delivery ensured that evolving needs and suggestions from stakeholders were absorbed and the MIS project adapted accordingly. As an indicator of the scale of this process, there were over 500 stakeholder engagement meetings, which yielded more than 700 pieces of feedback, leading to more than 200 system changes. By involving lines of business in this process of prototyping, stress-testing and refining the solution, a group of advocates within the organisation was created.

Principle 4 – Ease of use

The MIS has been designed to be intuitive and simple to ensure it achieves high levels of adoption. There are over 400 active users globally, meaning it has embedded itself into decision-making.

Principle 5 – Fun

Gamification has been applied to the training programme for users, such as a quiz in which teams compete to discover features and functionality. To communicate how the MIS is supporting the company's commercial strategy, a town hall event was run themed around the British TV programme, *Blockbusters*. One UK manager said of their introduction to the system, "it was one of the best meetings I've ever had", while an analyst described a training session as, "a fab way to ensure everyone knows how to use a great tool!"

Aligning business strategy and data strategy

The DataIQ Way places particular emphasis on the alignment of business strategies and data strategies for a reason. If data and analytics are deployed only as part of business retooling, for example during a digital transformation, this creates a dependency on individuals and functions to adopt these resources.

As the Jaguar Land Rover example demonstrates, if business stakeholders support a new process, adoption will grow. But if there is any level of resistance, such as to protect a data 'fiefdom' or out of concerns that access to a habitual report or metric might be lost, then usage rates will be limited and patchy, rather than enterprise-wide and consistent. Typically, this can lead to the perception that data is a cost centre, with no visibility of any value that it is creating for the organisation – 15% of respondents to a DataIQ survey held this view.

By contrast, if there is close alignment between the business and data, the goals being pursued will inherently require these resources, and the execution of the business strategy will have data and analytics at its core. Moving towards this approach often requires senior leaders to advocate for evidence-based decision-making – 9.9% of organisations at the second level of maturity ('Data-driven') are using new technologies to make this happen, looking for better access to data to track their activities and increase the cycle time of their decisions.

Creating this desire for better resources will help to improve data maturity, but there remains the risk that it will only increase in those functions with a leader advocating for them – at the third level of maturity ('Data literate'), 23.9% say their decision-making is improving, but not across the whole organisation.

To be fully mature – a 'Data native' at the fifth level of maturity – there needs to be a fundamental reliance on data and analytics resources across the business operating model. Some 28% of organisations told DataIQ this was true at a skills level, although only 16% describe their maturity level as advanced. What this indicates is that data leaders will need to act continually as change agents until the enterprise culture has been fully transformed.

DataIQ Way Marker

Leaders are the key drivers of data and analytics, not technology

Developing use cases

Adoption of data is certainly strongest when there are clear benefits to individual users, teams, leaders and the organisation as a whole. While this might seem obvious at a behavioural level, it does create problems when the data office needs to argue for investment into foundational programmes that may not appear to deliver benefits directly, as we saw in Chapter 1 with the problem of crossing the data bridge. Activities such as data governance or master data management can lack the appeal to senior leaders which they find in self-service dashboards or AI, for example, yet they support those new projects at a foundational level and ensure they are more likely to succeed.

Specific use cases will be company-specific, but there are some generic drivers that can be applied to win investment. As a general rule, the argument breaks out into one of four categories of investment:

1. technology

2. headcount

3. toolkits

4. innovation.

Each of these has a different principle and set of risk and success factors at its heart which need to be carefully considered.

Technology investment – relatively straightforward as long as the use case can be substantiated and incremental gain demonstrated from automating a process or updating a technology platform. A strong business need should play a central part in the argument with clear before and after measures applied.

Principle: business enabler

Risk: poor or incomplete metrics

Success factor: demonstrating business returns

Headcount investment – harder to argue because of the increase in costs, which directly impacts on the bottom line. It should be recognised that there is even a personal dimension to this since senior executives often have their bonuses linked to the P&L. The focus of the business case should be its impact on incremental revenue, cost reduction or improved customer experience for which additional human resources in the data office are essential to manage the extra load. Involving stakeholders to support the argument for extra headcount is valuable. As one DataIQ Leaders member put it: *"Try to get them to do the ask."*

Principle: supporting transformation

Risk: getting the business to agree on the target and baseline

Success factor: engaging stakeholders

Toolkit investment – this is a strategic business case, rather than one focused on incremental gains. It identifies new IT-supported capabilities, such as moving into the cloud or creating a data platform. The investment required is large and the return is not always evident within the project itself. A good area to focus on is the replacement of sub-optimal tools, such as internally-built applications that have been superseded, or external solutions which are no longer supported. Sometimes this case can be made more powerfully in the wake of a project failure where the business needs to rethink its strategy.

Principle: strategic development

Risk: business had its fingers burned

Success factor: new generation replacement for legacy systems

Innovation investment – usually a less significant level of investment, innovation is essential to move the business forward and offers analytics the opportunity to find breakthrough solutions. In some businesses, innovation lives within a specific R&D department. Where this is not present, the argument should be for a specific percentage of programme budgets to be set aside for exploratory projects, generally between 5% and 30%.

Principle: future-focused, not business as usual (BAU)

Risk: often does not produce deliverables

Success factor: comparison with sector/industry competitors and disruptors

Winning approaches for the business case

Alongside the success factors identified for use cases above, there are additional components that the data leader can build into their argument which improve the likelihood of getting sign-off:

Financial specifics – all business cases are competing for the same investment pot, so the argument has to be made in the language of the business (i.e. financial). While costs are relatively easy to identify, benefits can be harder to prove as they happen downstream from data and analytics, often without direct metrics from any process change. Putting a number – any number – on the return on investment is essential.

Regulatory change – as was experienced with MiFID in the banking sector and GDPR across all organisations holding personal data, changes to the regulatory landscape unlock investment budgets. Moving early with a use case that addresses new regulations, while also building new data foundations, is a shrewd move but which can only usually be made once.

Executive focus – understanding what the board and C-suite are concerned about (through vision statements, internal comms and the like) creates leverage for a business case. New faces around the boardroom table are often prime moments for new business cases to be made, especially if an incoming CEO confirms the importance of data.

Stakeholder cheerleaders – as noted above, having a representative from a line of business argue for the need to invest in data is highly persuasive. This may provide a base for the whole investment needed, or it may be possible to create a coalition of stakeholders who each agree to provide support and 'donate' a percentage of the benefits that accrue as proofs of ROI.

Simple solutions – successful business cases are often those which the business finds easiest to imagine being delivered. A focus on simple solutions for pressing business problems is more likely to win backing as a result.

Obstacles for data and analytics business cases

Any pitch to the board is likely to face objections or obstacles. Recognising what these are likely to be in advance can help to prepare counter-arguments.

Outside the C-suite – in most organisations, data does not have a voice on the board and in many it does not even have an advocate. As a result, it can be easier for investment to be directed towards other projects coming from departments with which the business is more familiar.

Fear of change – humans tend to view change as a threat, so making the case for a data project that might transform processes, replace jobs (as with AI and automation) or even reduce bonuses may struggle to win support.

Behind the curve – while awareness of new techniques and tools, from big data through to AI and ML, may appear to be helpful for data investments, it may be too late to catch up by embarking on such projects by the time the C-suite has absorbed the concept.

Business myths – all organisations have beliefs about what makes them successful. Data often contradicts these myths with an evidence base for alternative explanations. But these organisational shibboleths tend to serve as the bases for political power which stakeholders may not be willing to give up.

Too clever by half – even in data native organisations, it is possible to propose new business projects which are simply over-complex or unlikely to be capable of being operationalised. Boards tend to take a helicopter view of the business and what will help it, with the consequence that they have a low tolerance of anything which cannot be explained simply.

―――――――――― **DataIQ Way Marker** ――――――――――

Make the use case in the language of business
– revenue, costs, ROI

Building skills in the organisation

At the very highest level of maturity when the organisation has become data native, it is because the use of data and analytics is fundamental to the way it operates. Reaching this state clearly requires the right skills to be inherent within everybody, from the senior leadership team through to junior representatives, from the front office to the back office. If the vision for the organisation requires these skills to be in place, then a focus on recruiting, developing and refreshing them is essential.

Viewing data skills as purely technical is a mistake, however. If the recruitment process is already filtering for numeracy at a basic level, talent management can layer in more specific requirements, such as coding languages or familiarity with mathematical and statistical techniques. Many of these will be specific to each role – not everybody across the enterprise needs to be able to write an analytical query, build a model or even visualise data.

What is essential to reach the level of data literacy and then progress to have a true data culture and ultimately become data native is an analytical mindset and understanding of concepts like test-and-learn. Alongside these will sit soft skills such as communication, engagement and even emotional intelligence. Translating business issues into the right questions and extrapolating from data to reach a decision are mental abilities as much as they are about possessing technical knowledge.

The future of jobs

A major reason for putting soft skills at the centre of talent management and career development strategies is the way in which employment is evolving. Data and analytics are themselves playing a huge part in this shift, not least by driving automation, and these functions will themselves be subject to the replacement of human skills, such as the use of ML-driven models for data extraction and preparation, for example.

The World Economic Forum report from 2018, *The Future of Jobs*, laid out from a macro perspective how skills are being impacted. Table 4.1 shows the types of skill in demand at the time the report was published and those expected to undergo a rise and fall within a five-year timescale to 2022. It is striking that eight of the top ten skills predicted to be trending are soft skills, behaviours and mindsets, while only two are technical (programming, systems analysis).

Table 4.1: Top ten skills in demand 2018 vs 2022

2018	Trending 2022	Declining 2022
Active thinking and innovation	Active thinking and innovation	Manual dexterity, endurance and precision
Complex problem-solving	Active learning and learning strategies	Memory, verbal, auditory and spatial abilities
Critical thinking and analysis	Creativity, originality and initiative	Management of financial and material resources
Active learning and learning strategies	Technology design and programming	Technology installation and maintenance
Creativity, originality and initiative	Critical thinking and analysis	Reading, writing, maths and active listening
Attention to detail, trustworthiness	Complex problem-solving	Management of personnel
Emotional intelligence	Leadership and social influence	Quality control and safety awareness
Reasoning, problem-solving and ideation	Emotional intelligence	Coordination and time management
Leadership and social influence	Reasoning, problem-solving and ideation	Visual, auditory and speech abilities
Coordination and time management	Systems analysis and evaluation	Technology use, monitoring and control

Source: WEF, *The Future of Jobs*, 2018

The trends identified by WEF appear to present as much of a threat to middle management as they do to manual workers (and potentially creative industries, too). As noted earlier, much of this derives from the increasing use of automation which will impact even on the data space as machine-to-machine learning allows for tasks such as data management to be handed off to tools, which will typically be cloud-based. Where the impact will be at its lowest, however, is in the leadership space and around the actions taken by data analysts in their roles as trusted advisers (see Figure 4.1). Providing they have the right learning strategies in place to maintain their advantage, that is.

Figure 4.1: Ratio of human-machine working hours, 2018 vs 2022 (projected)

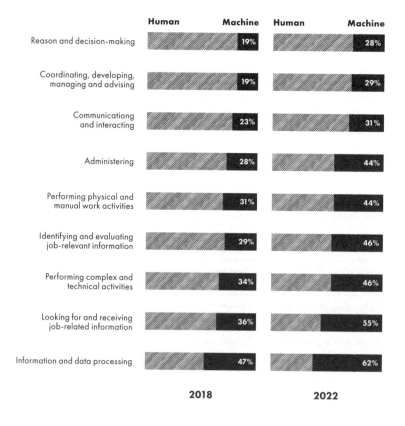

——————— **DataIQ Way Marker** ———————

Skills need to reflect the culture and maturity level desired

▼

Creating a skills map

Given the dynamism of skills demanded both in the macro employment market and the micro requirements of each organisation, it is essential to have a skills map in place that addresses current and future needs. If this is only done to address immediate demands created by the tasks on hand, it will support BAU but will not serve to progress the maturity of the organisation or future-proof its culture. There is also the risk of reinforcing silos by embedding skills within localised roles or limiting the skills available in those roles to a specific set of tasks.

Development is only possible when the skillset exceeds the current requirement and can be leveraged for innovation. Assessing how well the skills, present across the data department and within teams, map against the strategic goals of the business, using a tool such as DataIQ CARBON™, can help to provide a strong indicator of where additional support is needed or new opportunities are capable of being tackled.

The opportunity to progress the organisation's culture and maturity can be identified within the skills map itself, especially if it is structured around job families and hierarchies. This perspective will show where there is duplication of abilities which can be thinned out or if skills are available, but not being used, which can be applied to new areas. A significant upside of this approach is the ability to maintain a rolling 12-month cycle of skills development that informs HR-led recruitment tactics and internal investment into re-skilling and up-skilling.

Without this forward focus, organisations can find themselves stuck at level one of maturity with no view as to what skills they will need even at the one-year horizon, let alone three to five years out. Even those at level two are typically only considering their skills requirement within the current 12-month cycle, rather than considering what will be needed next once open roles have been filled and new hires have begun their career progression, as well as how to build out capabilities beyond current tasks.

As the data resource grows and becomes more capable, needs will open up that can begin to be identified some distance out. This is typical of level three maturity, where recruitment is looking both at its current needs and also making ad hoc guesses at what it will need to recruit for in the next 12-month cycle.

Maturity of skills really only dawns at level four ('Data cultured') with a rolling horizon for one year out, planning what needs will be addressed next year while recruiting and training for this year, rather than waiting to be within that window before deciding. This is clearly a more planned and structured approach that can also be applied to developing existing practitioners in the second or third years, as well as identifying where managers and leaders need to be planning to build on their skills base. Once this horizon line gets set at a distance of two to three years – aligned with business strategy planning and recognising the potential to develop talent within apprenticeships or while still pursuing graduate studies – the company will be at level five ('Data native').

Structured learning and development

Career development and learning plans are a relatively new concept within the data space. Overheated demand for these skills has tended to create an emphasis on recruiting into target roles rather than on maintaining and building up the skillset within incumbent practitioners. Where there is either no significant HR resource or support available (as is the case in many SMEs), or HR has not fully engaged with the data and analytics officers, this can place a burden on the CDO to put structured learning programmes in place.

For that reason, self-learning often fills the skills gap. This may be suitable for technical skills since most technology vendors have extensive training programmes that can be accessed online. Making time for this within working hours is one way to structure and control how this is pursued – the risk is that individuals will choose to learn skills that suit their own interests, rather than what will support the goals of the business.

When putting in place more formal learning plans, it is important to add soft skills development alongside technical skills. While it is tempting to see broader coding abilities or fresh techniques as the path to higher productivity, they will not achieve this goal unless they are harnessed to the ability to understand stakeholders, translate their needs into technical specifications, manage projects end-to-end and deliver them back in a way that the business can absorb and benefit from (see the next section for more on this).

Depending on the level of resource and timeline for a data literacy programme, this learning and development pathway can be developed in-house, which typically requires several years to create, or can be bought in from an external business partner with a level of bespoking depending on budget. It is worth considering that data academies require a lot of commitment and resourcing – it can be hard to maintain the momentum and typically such programmes get abandoned several years after they are initiated. A commercial partner has a vested interest in ensuring they maintain their assets and keep them fresh.

Align

Engaging stakeholders

If the ambition is to embed a data culture that may ultimately lead to the organisation being data native, then at its core the organisation will need non-specialist business leaders and managers who instinctively look for the tools and processes that support evidence-based decision-making. Outside of digitally native companies and start-ups, few will start from this point. Instead, the stakeholders of the data department need to be won around to the benefits and advantages of a new way of working.

For the data department itself, the goal of engaging with stakeholders in a new way is two-fold:

- To move away from operating as a reactive service provider.

- To establish the function as a trusted adviser and business partner.

Four habits of effective engagement

Over the course of conversations with more than 70 data practitioners drawn from 27 different organisations, DataIQ identified four habits which can ensure that the analytics team engages properly with its business stakeholders and delivers against their needs and expectations.

Habit 1 – Collaborating

Data is a contact sport – when data practitioners interact regularly with lines of business, ideas are exchanged, opportunities identified and the temperature of the business as a whole is better understood. A collaborative data leader will also benefit from being perceived as a trusted adviser and the provider of data which is a source of truth. This is especially the case if it is clear that feedback is welcomed and acted on.

Partnering data practitioners with specific business executives, either through routine meetings or by embedding them into the line of business itself, is the sign of a highly collaborative team. Collaboration tools are a key enabler for this habit.

Habit 2 – Communicating

Data can appear to its internal customers as something of a 'black box' which generates models through an invisible, quasi-magical process. Often, this is a direct consequence of limited communication by the data team with its stakeholders. Effective communication means adopting the terms and language of the business, rather than expecting business executives to understand the technical language of data.

Data storytelling and data visualisation are key tools in this process to translate the numerical process of data analysis into a language-based narrative which stakeholders can understand. A further step is essential – making the link between what the data team has done and successful business outcomes. It is often assumed that simply doing good work will lead to recognition by internal customers. But this is very rarely the case – those stakeholders need to be constantly informed, educated and reminded of how central data is to the success of their own line of business.

Habit 3 – Championing

A key role for the data department is to champion what it can do for the business, solving current problems and identifying opportunities. While there may already be top-down buy-in to the use of data to optimise processes and support new ones, this cannot be taken for granted.

Instead, it is important habitually to get behind the big issues. All CEOs have a list of priorities for the organisation which they intend to address. Typically, these will include cost reduction or incremental revenue, but might also cover sustainability, diversity, customer experience and more. If the data leader can champion these goals and offer support and solutions, it will reduce the risk of becoming exposed as a cost centre, rather than being recognised as a value-driver.

There are two aspects of this which can be difficult for a CDO: honesty and refusal. True champions are willing to admit when something is wrong or has not worked, while committing to discovering why this has happened and putting it right. Learning to say no is also the mark of a champion. This means closing down requests that are outside of agreed parameters or which can be shown to hold little real benefit. It also means admitting not knowing the answer in every circumstance. Showing a positive attitude towards such gaps and a keenness to close them as swiftly as possible will gain support and build real authority.

Habit 4 – Challenging

One of the toughest habits for the data department to adopt – especially more junior data team members – is that of challenging the business within which they work, especially when it is a senior executive they need to contradict. Yet without this behaviour, the department will only ever be reactive, rather than a proactive change agent.

The need to act in this way is probably most apparent in relation to the myths which tend to propagate across organisations. Examples of this might be a belief about 'hero products' (believed to be lynchpins of customer buying which may not actually perform in that way), the typical customer profile, what the real profitability of a service is and so forth. Typically, these grow unchallenged and become the basis for the political power of one line of business which happens to own these successes.

Once data practitioners get to work examining the available data, they will often uncover contradictory truths. This is especially true of data science if it is given free licence to look at the organisation end-to-end. Few of those business myths survive this examination.

It is the mark of a mature data department – and of the organisation that hosts it – when it becomes able to behave in this way. Relatively few functions have achieved this status as yet. But one of the key steps towards challenging in this way involves the use of data. Giving access via self-service tools can help because it quickly surfaces the reality of any given issue. As one DataIQ Leader put it: "Give them the rope and they will either skip or hang."

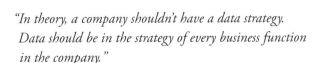

———— DataIQ Way Marker ————

Ensure data is not an ivory tower, but a beacon of truth

"In theory, a company shouldn't have a data strategy. Data should be in the strategy of every business function in the company."
– Lorenzo Bavasso, data, analytics and AI director, BT Global

Supporting business strategy

Data strategy is a key component of how the data office enables the processes and needs of the organisation. But it should not be an end in its own right – there is no benefit in creating the perfect data strategy unless it leads to positive effects, such as improved business performance, reduced costs, increased customer revenues or innovation. That is why the data strategy not only needs to align with the business strategy, but the business strategy needs to be developed with the data strategy at its heart, rather than layering data on top once it has been agreed.

If the data and analytics function has achieved the status of trusted adviser, then alignment can be achieved by ensuring the voice of data is present during strategy meetings. Where this is not yet the case, there are behaviours that can be adopted and actions to take which can start to bring about closer alignment. Reaching this state is not easy, however. In DataIQ research, 59% of organisations have not aligned their data strategy with the business strategy.

Drivers of alignment between data and business strategies

Achieving the best possible fit between these two can be delivered through a focus on five behaviours:

Vision – at all times, there should be a clear, consistent and well-communicated view from within the data office of how it will benefit the organisation and where it is aiming to lead it. This may be developed from a list of identified projects which need to be prioritised according to the business strategy, or it may be a more cultural goal. Maintaining the vision keeps the data department aligned and engaged with the business.

Leadership – as outlined earlier in the four habits of effective stakeholder engagement, the CDO can provide leadership to the organisation by championing and challenging. This will establish a habit of recognising that data is a core competency and support for the business strategy.

Stakeholder orientation – getting something right for a business stakeholder increases their perception of the data leader's value. This is more likely to happen if the business issue is thought through from the perspective of the line of business, rather than on the basis of which techniques, technologies or data sources will be appropriate. There are always multiple options to reach the same outcomes, albeit with differing levels of difficulty. Data teams should not shy away from a solution because it will be harder to deliver if it is a better fit for the stakeholder, whether from a cost, technology, timescale or value perspective. Constantly communicating examples of successful projects and outcomes across the business will reinforce the recognition that the function is stakeholder-oriented.

Domain knowledge – the data department needs to live by the saying, 'If you want to go fast, go alone. If you want to go far, go together.' Practitioners need to get close to the stakeholders they support in order to understand their needs, concerns and even internal politics. Domain knowledge takes time to build but can be built into the rules of engagement for the department with its internal clients.

Technical competence – the data office may start out with data quality goals, mature through broader governance and even become a 'Ministry of Truth' whose authority guarantees the credibility of any data source. At each stage, it is demonstrating the necessary skills to gain confidence from stakeholders.

Challenges to alignment

There are common challenges that arise which can delay or even prevent trusted advisor status being achieved and being invited into the development of the business strategy. These include:

Data evangelism – it is easy for data practitioners to become absorbed in their own self-belief that their data or model is the best and only solution for the business. This can come across as confrontational if analysts are contradicting executives who have many years of experience in the organisation, for example.

Poor communication – good data with a bad explanation is worse than bad data. Data literacy among non-technical executives is still relatively low and it is for the data department to explain clearly in the language of the business, rather than for the business to learn the terms and techniques of data.

Unrealistic expectations – both the data department and its stakeholders can become excited by the prospect of leading-edge projects, but these are not always appropriate to pursue. For example, the organisation may want to launch an AI initiative without having first developed consistent data definitions and data standards that will support such a project.

Advance

DataIQ Way Marker

Be restless

"Changing behaviour is less a matter of giving people analysis to influence their thoughts than helping them to see a truth to influence their feelings."

– John Kotter

The art of the possible

Adopting data is usually done as part of a wider change programme, such as a digital transformation. This gives it a robust context, parameters and goals within which to work and establish itself.

What happens next is what typically happens in all transformations – by year two, what seemed radical has become BAU and by year three, market conditions have changed in ways that alter the frame of reference for the change programme. The result? Organisations stop seeing the potential for innovation offered by data and may even start to question the return on investment being delivered.

Evidence for the risk of stalling in this way is easy to find. When Nesta, the UK's innovation thinktank, carried out research in 2012, it found that only 18% of UK plcs could be classified as Datavores – companies that were making optimal use of the digital data they possessed through the application of advanced analytics. By 2020, when DataIQ surveyed 103 leading end-user organisations, only 16% described themselves as advanced. One study by McKinsey identified that 70% of change programmes fail to achieve the impact that was expected.

One area where this becomes particularly visible is in the job tenure of CDOs – among the 28 CDOs who featured in the 2018 edition of the DataIQ 100, 12 had moved to a different organisation by 2019. Frustration with the slow rate of maturity of data alongside shifting rules of engagement often combine to push a former data champion away from their business. Even worse, the incoming CDO will often disavow their predecessor's work – usually to neutralise any potential political damage – thereby downshifting the overall level of maturity, or taking the organisation in a different direction.

A similar effect can result from changes elsewhere in the C-suite, especially if a senior executive who was a key sponsor for data leaves the business. Under a previous CEO, one of the largest insurance providers in the UK invested extensively into data and analytics. It established a stand-alone digital operation with the culture of a start-up that was very distinct from the more traditional head office. This is a sector that is very risk-averse, yet the new function created in 2016 was given a mission to "put a rocket up the company". To accelerate its impact, 70 data scientists were recruited and tasked to "move fast and break things".

Significant changes did start to be realised, including a reduction in the friction during insurance pricing and quotation through predictive modelling based on customer data. Robust data underpinnings and platforms were put in place to support both customer science and data science with strong growth in internal demand as business units – which had been set against each other to create a competitive culture – looked for support for ongoing innovation and optimisation.

Despite all of this progress, a new CEO arrived in 2019 who had a more traditional view and set about reviewing the business benefits being derived from data. Although there was clearly a potential culture clash, one of the senior leaders in the digital operation recognised that the data function needed to help the CEO understand what it could do for the business, having already taken it from zero up a steep learning curve. That would involve continuing to do great work and also good internal PR in order to maintain momentum.

> *"A paradigm shift occurs when a question is asked inside the current paradigm that can only be answered from outside it."*
> **– Marilee Goldberg from *The Art of the Question***

Looking over the horizon

If the data office is genuinely to advance its position within the organisation, then this is only possible by looking beyond current requirements and the immediate to-be demands. A horizon line of three to five years out needs to be set – this will establish data as a visionary department, not just a service provider.

The art of the possible is central to this approach. If analytics is about asking the right questions, the CDO needs to enable stakeholders to ask about things they have assumed to be out of scope. In this way, behaviour begins to change and innovation becomes feasible.

To do this requires a recognition that humans are driven more by emotion than reason. In the context of digital transformations and the data projects supporting them, this typically produces three major phases:

- *See* – compelling and eye-catching situations are created to help show people what the problems are and how to resolve them.

- *Feel* – visualising ideas evokes a powerful emotional response that motivates people into action.

- *Change* – the new feelings change behaviours and make people work harder to turn the vision into reality. Note that constant reinforcement is required to embed these new behaviours.

For this reason, the first two columns in Table 4.2 need to be given as much emphasis as the next three, even though these are typically the core areas of focus in a transformation.

Table 4.2: Five pillars of transformation

Culture and change	People	Data	Process	Technology
Recognition and rewards	Skills and capability audit	Type audit	Process audit	Internal IT benchmarking
Resilience	Role definition	Location audit	Testing	External benchmarking
Challenges	Competency assessment	Ownership	Process development	Capability assessment
"If you..., then I..."	Training	Integration	Process launch	Landscape review
Vision	Goals	Hidden data	Process retirement	Needs assessment
Decisions	Development	Classification	Data quality	Training
Support	Retention	Data dictionaries	Benchmarking	Performance assessment
Review and refocus	Recruitment and improvement	Rules and standards	Improvement and updating	Cost-benefit analysis

Towards the data native organisation

In its most advanced state of maturity, an organisation will reach the state of being data native. Chapter 3 laid out the roadmap towards this situation and the core elements of what such a business would look like.

Crucially, data will be part of the organisation's DNA, indistinguishable and inseparable from its operating model. The behaviours of everybody in the enterprise will be influenced, supported and measured by data – in fact, it will feel alien to colleagues if there is any decision-making or process that lacks this base.

With a strong leadership model, especially in an organisation that has external investors and stakeholders who expect constant adaptation, the drive towards this state can be maintained over the multi-year timeline it requires. By painting an optimistic picture of where the company will be in three years' time, it is possible to build sufficient internal energy to sustain the change management programme across that period.

Often, this is accompanied by an initial 'Moon shot project' to grab attention and demonstrate the new way in which data is intended to be used. The focus on this can be important as it will provide 'show, not tell' evidence that the new strategy is working. Equally, it is high risk because a) the project may not deliver the expected value and b) it will typically only benefit one part of the business if it does succeed.

Understandably, few organisations have achieved this outcome yet. In DataIQ research, the intersection between four key dimensions – transforming to be digital-first, data maturity, data literacy, alignment of data strategy with business strategy – was only occupied by two companies out of 103 surveyed. However, while one of these is a digital native, the other could be considered a legacy business. That indicates there are not necessarily any fundamental barriers to reaching data nirvana.

To understand what a data native organisation would feel like if you were working in one, consider the anecdote about a visit to NASA by President John F. Kennedy in 1962. On passing a janitor, he is reported to have asked the man what he was doing. The now famous reply came: "Mr President, I am helping to put a man on the moon."

Most commentary on this incident applauds the extent to which the janitor had bought into the vision of the organisation, seeing beyond his everyday tasks to the ultimate goal. But consider it the other way around – what happens to the vision if even the lowest role in a hierarchy does not buy in?

Good janitors make for clean workplaces. As the Covid-19 health crisis revealed, a virus can totally disrupt normal practice. And NASA knows this only too well – in February 1969, the Apollo 9 mission was delayed because the astronauts had caught a mild respiratory virus (or common cold). Current bio-security measures will undoubtedly have reduced a similar risk within contemporary aerospace establishments and would have eliminated the risk to those astronauts – hardly the fault of a 1960's janitor not to have lived in a time before hand sanitiser, but he would surely have kept dispensers topped up and surfaces clean given the option.

Building this level of culture requires a critical effort by leaders around sense-giving. This is the activity of helping employees to see and feel the connection between their work and the vision. This can be approached in four steps:

1. *Placing tasks in context* – explaining to every colleague how their daily activities map together, for example why an analyst needs to clean a data set in order for a model to be built.

2. *Connecting tasks to outcomes* – ensuring each colleague sees a result from their efforts, such as the analyst building a model that will increase marketing performance.

3. *Building towards a long-term objective* – giving a clear sequence of activities that will lead towards the big goal, such as the 'Moon shot' project that needs multiple supporting components.

4. *Turning the objective into the symbolic* – while getting to the moon was a specific long-term objective for NASA, it also aspired to advance science in ways that would support even longer-term goals, like going to Mars. Intangible, idealistic visions are easier to absorb at the symbolic level.

──────── **DataIQ Way Marker** ────────

Live the vision before it is launched

▼

DATA LITERACY STEPCOUNTER

The business is not waiting to find out how data can help it – it needs to be told.

Neither is it always wanting to become data literate – it needs to be shown why this makes the business strategy more achievable.

Steps 10–13:

10. Ensure use cases and investment pitches have a clear benefit for the business in financial terms.

11. Assess existing skills and map both the current and future needs.

12. Develop the right habits to build engagement with stakeholders and maintain alignment between the data strategy and the business strategy.

13. Find a 'Moon shot' that embodies the leading edge of what data could do for the organisation in order to 'show, not tell'.

CHAPTER 5

Building a data culture

Roadmap – in this chapter:

- Failure to align data definitions and KPIs can lead to disaster – just ask NASA.

- Openreach and Public Health England used BI to drive performance improvements.

- Creating a common data asset is essential but difficult due to political resistance.

- To avoid misalignment of definitions, data governance should be maintained from the centre.

- The ultimate objective should be for the brand to live its values in its use of data, including AI ethics.

Democratise

DataIQ Way Marker

Create a data 'Ministry of Truth'

Data as the single source of truth

As the examples of Aviva and Jaguar Land Rover in earlier chapters have shown, BI can be the catalyst for driving transformation and maturity in the use of data. Having access to consistent, reliable, real-time indicators of performance can make the difference between a positive strategic outcome and a negative tactical reaction. That is a powerful way to get buy-in from senior executives and stakeholders across the organisation.

But there is a problem.

BI, in the form of dashboards and reports, is one of the most contested and political arenas for data. Individual departments may consider a data item to belong to themselves, rather than viewing it as a company asset. Individuals may be incentivised or rewarded based on existing KPIs – if these are changed, it can hit their pocket.

As any user of BI during critical meetings will know, however, failure to achieve alignment across all of these key indicators causes problems and even flawed decision-making. At a basic level, inconsistencies in data definitions and descriptions can lead to disputes about which number is the 'real' one. It may even have a catastrophic impact.

The best-known example of this was the 1999 Mars Orbiter mission by NASA. After a 286-day journey from Earth, the probe was due to enter the planet's orbit at a height of 160 km. Instead, it arrived at a height of 60 km – when its engines were fired, it sent the orbiter through the atmosphere and beyond the planet, losing the $125 million scientific project.

The cause of this disaster was conflict between two data definitions. The probe's manufacturer Lockheed Martin was using the imperial measurement system of feet and inches, while NASA was using the metric system of metres and centimetres. This mismatch prevented navigation data from transferring between the Mars Orbiter team working for Lockheed Martin and NASA's flight team. Commenting at the time, the project leader said: "This is an end-to-end process problem. A single error like this should not have caused the loss of Climate Orbiter. Something went wrong in our system processes in checks and balances that we have that should have caught this and fixed it."

If that sounds familiar, then it is – a common feature of business meetings is the disagreement about the numbers being presented and why they don't reconcile or accord with what had been expected. In DataIQ research, 84.5% of firms say that common data definitions are essential for data integration – the number one issue they identify.

Tackling this is often the entry point for a new data department and its CDO. By aligning data definitions and addressing master data management, BI and reporting emerges as a reliable asset. Giving data authority helps to build the status of the CDO and gives the data department a position as the 'Ministry of Truth'.

How Openreach and Public Health England used BI to drive performance improvements

The impact of building a single source of data which is fully integrated and to the right standard can be significant. In 2016, Openreach was facing growing pressure from two directions at once – the customer base for its business networking services and Ofcom, the regulator which oversees the telecoms and ISP sector. The reason was poor operational performance when installing ethernet, a key product line for larger businesses. Customer satisfaction was measured using

Net Promoter Score (NPS) – at the time, Openreach had a rating of minus 100, the lowest possible score.

An underlying cause of the problem was installations that were taking more than 140 working days to complete, well in excess of both Openreach's target and industry averages. While a backlog of work meant ongoing delays in closing these open tickets, the way data was being captured and analysed was also not helpful. Business analysts were using Excel, which has inherent limits on the volume of data it is able to store and also in managing and sharing versions of spreadsheets. Migrating to a modern BI tool not only made the data more accessible and presented it in a user-friendly way, it also surfaced a critical root cause.

As Jason Teoh, then head of business intelligence at Openreach's fibre and network delivery division, noted at the time: "One of the things analysts started to understand was that it was not just about those overdue jobs, but also about the ones running at between 100 and 140 days. If they could stop those going over the threshold, it would help. It was the first time they had been able to look at the problem from a different perspective."

Once Openreach had got the work queue down from several thousand to several hundred overdue jobs, it started to develop other ways of using analytics that hadn't been thought of before. By 2017, the impact of this new approach was beginning to be felt, with the average job time reduced from 75 to 35 working days overall. The operations team was also able to reduce the stack of extremely overdue jobs, pulling the average down to meet the regulatory target. The NPS also rose significantly to plus 30.

An almost identical issue occurred within Public Health England during the Covid-19 crisis of 2020. Multiple test outcomes were being compiled using Excel, but back-checking identified that nearly 16,000 positive cases had not been recorded and passed to the Track and Trace service. The cause was an issue with the spreadsheet application in which older versions (.XLS) had a 65,536 row limit, compared to the 1 million-plus limit in the newest version (.XLSX). Importing new results into the older version led to many simply being left off when the row limit was reached.

In a commercial environment, the consequences of a similar data problem arising are likely to involve revisiting decisions and investment plans as numbers get reviewed and corrected. That undermines the credibility of the data and the commitment of senior executives and managers to using BI, rather than instinct or gut feel.

Data as a shared asset

If data is kept in silos within individual departments under the jealous guardianship of each business leader, it may well benefit them and their specific processes. However, it will not enable enterprise-wide processes, innovation or enhanced value for customers and the organisation.

Even those companies with the best of intentions around managing their data can struggle to build a single, consistent, coherent and governed view of their customers. Where there is no overarching strategy to become customer-centric, the problem of data silos multiplies further – the UK's largest insurance provider, operating across 27 separate brands, was still holding records by policy, not customer in 2018. A mobile telephone network operator still holds 16 separate copies of its call records, none of which match.

Table 5.1 summarises the experience of DataIQ Leaders members. It shows the diversity of data management approaches, but with common features such as departments or brands creating their own silos within both data and technology. As organisations grow, so do the challenges – in one case, the fundraising platform saw its daily event logs rise from 20,000 to 2bn per day, for example.

Table 5.1: DataIQ Leaders' data silo issues

Organisation type	Data management challenge
B2B publisher	• Multiple brands operate independent databases • Each brand operates own technology stack • Not perceived as silos as no central oversight to recognise the issue • Five failed attempts to build an SCV to date
B2C publisher	• 30 brands each with independent databases • 'Random' adoption of data management technology by each brand • 49 third-party systems in use (excluding analytics and data sharing) • Privacy concerns driving pursuit of single view of subscribers
Fundraising platform	• Multiple data silos within functions • Recent acquisition by US software vendor has added 40 additional systems
Fundraising organisation	• Multiple data silos within functions with three main databases – legacy, supporters, volunteers • Implemented an SCV several years ago, but chose the wrong solution, which does not operate as expected • Creating specific views on top of silos to support specified needs
Insurance provider	• Data transformation in process • Intending to create single view of customers • Focus on eliminating 'shadow' IT • Has moved data science entirely away from the IT function
Membership service	• Data transformation in progress • Intending to create single view of customers • Privacy roadmap created, but policies and processes lagging
Professional intermediary (energy, finance)	• Multiple data silos following merger and acquisition • Global governance strategy • Global view of appropriate location for data management based on regulatory frameworks
Property services group	• 50 brands each with independent databases • Each brand operates own technology stack • Data governance has been centralised
Retail bank	• Single view of customers in place • Focus on ingesting data through GDPR portability • Open data strategy • Data infrastructure migrating to cloud
Subscription-based broadcaster	• Single view of subscribers in place • Content developers looking to access subscriber data to drive personalisation • Governance focus driving adoption of single view

The organisation needs to choose the boundaries within which its data is shared, but these should certainly be beyond a single department (unless there is a regulatory reason for tight control). Assigning responsibility and authority to a data office, especially under the supervision of a CDO, is a critical first step in building a true data asset that is shareable.

In economic terms, these benefits from shared data are called 'externalities'. Their value goes beyond the specific action for which the data was first intended – it extends not only across the organisation but potentially into the whole economy and society. If that seems fanciful, then consider the externalities from an individual health record, for example. Each patient experiences personalised treatment and a more efficient and effective service if that data is available to any healthcare professional who needs it. If that patient data is also available externally to the healthcare system (subject to specific, rigorous controls and anonymisation), the ability for researchers to combine it into disease-specific models or for policymakers to consider various scenarios for intervention and support creates significant externality value.

Other sectors are recognising the potential value of data sharing, especially those with extended supply chains. Agriculture is a case in point – it generates more data than any other industry. However, 62% of farmers do not collect and share data. The UK construction sector is responsible for projects with a value of more than £150bn each year, but there is very limited data sharing between the parties involved, leading to significant negative impacts. A survey of 12,000 major construction projects found that only 0.5% of them deliver their defined benefits on time and within budget. Data, and the intelligent insight from analytics, could drive improvement with large-scale returns. The Project Data Analytics Task Force (PDATF) has pulled together representatives from over 70 companies in this sector and outlined a vision that includes democratising data-driven solutions, agreeing data standards and facilitating data access.

Data sharing as a project within a single organisation should be approached in the same way: creating a project team comprising cross-departmental stakeholders, identifying the critical data sets to be integrated and shared, setting out a charter around which the project will cohere. In this way, a sense of shared ownership and mutual benefit is baked into the data asset from the outset.

This also helps to ensure that data is freely democratised, rather than only those items which appear relevant to the data department at the time. Di Mayze, global head of data and AI at global marketing services group WPP, has a telling anecdote about this process: "Data variety is front and centre of our data strategy which means that we are democratising hundreds of data sets (and not just to analysts!), some of which seem irrelevant until a different lens is put on them. My favourite example of this is sharing a data set about raptors and whether you would have been killed by one depending on where you lived. 'I love all data, but have to admit this is probably pretty useless,' I said during one presentation internally. 'Oh no, this is great,' said a colleague. 'We are just working on a project around Jurassic Park and this data set is perfect.' So you really never know what data set is gold dust!"

Centralised governance, federated analytics

In providing the business with wide-ranging data access, there is a risk that self-created reports and insights might be based on false assumptions or flawed data. Part of the goal of data literacy is to drive up overall numeracy in order to help avoid simple errors in statistics or in understanding how they are presented.

This is where the data department has an important role to play by setting standards and vetting models before they become widely disseminated. In fact, building out a library of models can be a core enabler of self-service BI or analytics by removing both the toil and the risk involved. Vendors of these enabling solutions typically have pre-built libraries that can accelerate this process.

Similarly, governance has to be kept in a central function and operated as the gatekeeper for any data source being admitted into the self-service environment. Chaos is likely to ensue unless data sets conform to the right standards, definitions, permissions and lineage, also serving to undermine the benefits of data democracy because unregulated data will not align across the enterprise in the desired way.

In reverse, there is also a gain to be made from keeping data centralised. One multi-line insurance provider was struggling with data democratisation because of the risk that users could misinterpret BI if they were not data literate and numerate, for example. But equally, there was a need to get data scientists to understand the commercial business. It had 30 data scientists who needed to make things "painfully simple" for business users, rather than following their natural desire to explain the supporting techniques. They also needed to recognise that they didn't understand the business as well as their stakeholders.

Develop

DataIQ Way Marker

Have everybody speak a common data language

Creating a common data language

Progress towards being data native needs to be supported by an evolving data culture, the next step on from achieving data literacy.

Central to this data culture is a common language spoken across the organisation by the stakeholders in data and analytics outputs and the practitioners creating them. This has the same potential impact as agreeing data definitions – when both sides use a term with a shared meaning, it accelerates the process from ideation to deployment.

For this reason, organisations looking to develop their maturity are increasingly focused on soft skills development. The focus of these learning programmes is on developing the skills that help a team transform from just analysing and reporting to storytelling the 'so what?' of data.

Walgreens Boots Alliance (WBA) identified a need for this breadth of soft skills within its global insight team which needed to be able to communicate the critical elements of consumer and customer insight in a fact-based, objective, compelling and believable way to diverse audiences. The approach adopted by WBA identified seven skills areas and four levels of ability that it needed to work across, as set out in its 'Knowhow framework' (see Table 5.2).

Table 5.2: WBA Knowhow framework

	Foundation	Competent	Expert	Authority
Business understanding				
Market understanding				
Internal partnering				
External partnering				
Technical mastery				
Generating exceptional understanding				
Synthesis, judgement and communication				

WBA saw that its global insights team could provide transformative outputs if it were better able to communicate with business stakeholders. As a first step, ways of working were identified and trained within the team to create an aligned, consistent approach via a shared culture in the global insight team. This was then enhanced with external workshops for leaders of lines of business around the same framework and concepts to embed a common language.

A growing number of organisations have identified a similar need and are moving to create cross-departmental courses that allow everybody to learn, adopt and deploy new data and analytics skills. Data science is a prime example. There is a large appetite from the C-suite down to bring leading-edge techniques, such as AI and ML, to bear on business problems.

The first obstacle for non-experts in understanding this area of practice is that these are complex concepts which require an understanding of multiple disciplines, including data, coding and mathematics. In DataIQ research, for example, 39.5% of data practitioners identified a weak understanding of data science in their business as the number one challenge they face.

But these concepts are teachable when broken down into digestible components that build towards a coherent framework. Involving academic institutions who have the necessary educational skills is one way in which commercial organisations are approaching this aspect of learning and development.

NatWest Group started its data academy – the first one to be launched by a UK bank – initially with a data science course, working with the Bayes Centre in Edinburgh to build a community of practice across the group. It set a clear goal of developing techniques, tools and also personal development pathways to allow it to drive innovation and be at the leading edge of disruptive data trends. To do this, it needed to move data science higher up the value chain by training its analysts to automate basic tasks, deliver self-service data tools and support the rollout of AI initiatives.

Over time, more courses and pathways have been added as part of a £2 million investment which has allowed 600 data and analytics practitioners and over 4,000 non-data staff to up-skill themselves. Business benefits have been realised on the back of this activity, for example from the ML engineer nano-degree that was introduced. One practitioner on the course built an ML model to score personal loan applications that was deployed by the risk department. It proved to be 17% more predictive than the existing model and would increase loan acceptances by 2.6%, yielding a potential benefit of £35 million over five years.

Deepen

―――――――――――― **DataIQ Way Marker** ――――――――――――

Data native brands have data as part of the brand promise

▼

Embedding data into the brand

One of the most powerful ways to ensure data is supporting the organisation's vision is to explore where the values and strengths of the brand intersect with the data strategy. This is visible in the context of data ethics and AI ethics. When developing a framework for these, consideration needs to be given to how this will be lived in the operational environment as this is where customers and prospects directly experience the brand.

From the data requested and the way the privacy policy is written and presented, through to how risk models are built and services personalised, data native brands present a seamless proposition that avoids dissonance between stated intentions and delivered behaviours.

To establish a common data language and embed shared concepts in the business and brand, the data department first needs to listen to the business. When GSK Consumer Healthcare was developing the data strategy for the new division, it first conducted a data maturity survey across 100 business leaders, as well as face-to-face interviews with 35 key stakeholders.

As a result of the listening exercise that was carried out, the data department identified a lack of access to data resources and a skills gap that was creating frustration. To resolve this, as well as building a self-service data platform, it has introduced a data literacy skills programme that extends skills and knowledge outside of the data function, including across the C-suite.

It is through putting such enablers in place that a data-driven mindset can emerge. Data literacy leading to a data culture will ensure that the way the brand behaves aligns with the way it uses data. In the optimal state, behaviours across the organisation reflect the policies that are in place without the need for overt controls and monitoring.

DATA LITERACY STEPCOUNTER

Trust is a foundation stone of a thriving data culture – the enterprise needs to have trust in all of its data.

Common language and core skills need to be embedded and aligned with the brand's values.

Steps 14–18:

14. Create a roadmap towards an integrated, centralised data asset.

15. Agree common data definitions and embed these into KPIs and reports.

16. Centralise data governance to maintain alignment across data sources.

17. Introduce data literacy programmes to enhance understanding across the organisation.

18. Ensure brand values are lived within data processes and the data strategy.

CHAPTER 6
Data leaders

Roadmap – in this chapter:

- Leading a data department differs from conventional management because data practitioners differ from conventional workers.

- Data leaders need to develop their social capital and positive politics as part of their T-shaped skills.

- Understanding Career Anchors – personal goals and working styles – will help to set the data leader's approach.

- The data department needs to be managed for its productivity, financial contribution and costs, just like any other. Hard and soft metrics are needed to support this.

- Momentum behind the adoption of data – including becoming data literate – needs to be maintained by the data leader regardless of changes in the boardroom.

- Personal growth and talent growth go hand-in-hand as the data department expands.

Lead

"If you want to build a ship, don't drum up the men to
gather wood, divide the work and give orders.
Instead, teach them to yearn for the vast and endless sea."
– Antoine de Saint-Exupéry

Leadership in the data world

T HE CONCEPT OF leadership, as opposed to management, can be hard to pin down. One useful quote is often attributed to the management guru Peter Drucker: "Management is about getting people to do things right. Leadership is about getting people to do the right things."

This is a nuanced view that is worth deliberating, especially in the context of leading a data department. Conventional management has a view of processes as fixed with a straight line between initiation and outcome. Good management therefore becomes a matter of ensuring everybody sticks to the process as closely as possible – doing things right. The origins of this point of view are clearly in manufacturing and manual labour where production lines have fixed processes and where any deviation leads to expensive errors and delays.

In service industries, especially those employing knowledge workers (a term coined by Drucker in 1959 in his book, *Landmarks of Tomorrow*), it is hard to apply such management when there is no predetermined process to follow. Data often relies on a degree of test-and-learn and fail fast in order to reach the appropriate end point. Even then, it is likely that a data set or a model will be subject to constant iteration and optimisation. Sticking at it to achieve the best outcome and recognising the need for continuous improvement is about doing the right thing.

A key distinction between traditional workers and knowledge workers stems from this – instead of being subordinates to a boss, they are associates. Drucker tackled the shift in approach this requires in his 1999 book, *Management Challenges for the 21st Century*, where he noted that: "Knowledge workers must know more about their job than their boss does – or else they are no good at all. In fact, that they know more about their job than anybody else in the organisation is part of the definition of knowledge workers."

In recognising that data practitioners are likely to know more about their work – and certainly to be more technically proficient than the data leader – it is clear that a different approach to leading such individuals and teams is required. A data leader cannot simply tell people what to do when they do not know the full complexity of what is involved. That is one reason why the agile methodology has gained significant traction in this sector, as it is inherently based on the idea of iterative development.

Instead, data leadership is more demanding of soft skills and people management than it is of technical ability and process adherence. This involves four key areas of focus:

1. *Nurture motivation* – instead of conventional leadership, where motivation is created from the top by the leader and fed into individuals and teams, the data leader must understand what motivates each practitioner and ensure this flame is kept alight.

2. *Represent externally* – being visible outside of the immediate domain of influence, whether across the wider organisation or beyond in the industry. This is the one area that draws on conventional leadership, although the nature of the engagement will differ in being more focused on thought leadership activities and representing data interests at the most senior level.

3. *Provide internal facilitation* – a data leader does not just decide and then project manage through to completion. They must create the right environment and support for data practitioners

to apply their competency and technical skills. Often, this involves the leader ensuring practitioners are protected from political pressure or excessive demands.

4. *Manage ambiguity* – the single biggest area of difference between data leadership, knowledge worker leadership and conventional management comes from the need to cope with non-binary outcomes and forecasts. Data routinely yields nuanced insights and ambiguous decision points which are for business leaders and senior executives to act on – the data leader must be able to explain the context and scenarios without yielding to pressure for overly simplified outputs.

────────── **DataIQ Way Marker** ──────────

Colleagues accept managers, but they seek leaders

▼

Social capital and positive politics

To achieve mastery of the four areas outlined above, the data leader has two major levers to pull on:

- Social capital
- Positive politics

Social capital

This term describes the extent and nature of our connections with others and the collective attitudes and behaviours between people that support a well-functioning, close-knit society. It is now considered to be so important to the well-being of a country that formal measurement is being taken, for example in the 25-indicator framework used by the Office of National Statistics in the UK that looks across national, local and individual engagement. An annual bulletin is released which tracks these indicators as an insight into shifting levels of trust, interaction and support.

As Eleanor Rees, head of social well-being analysis team at the ONS, commented when the initial release was published in February 2020: "Our social capital findings show that we are engaging less with our neighbours, but more with social media. We also note that we feel safer walking alone after dark in our neighbourhoods, but more recently fewer of us feel like we belong to them."

This concept of social capital can be readily transferred into the data department by converting national to organisational, local to departmental and retaining individual engagement as indicators. The target for the leader is to advance each of these metrics so that data becomes part of the enabling fabric of the business.

Positive politics

Alongside working on social capital, the data leader also needs to build their personal credibility across the business. Positive politics is the enabler for this. It involves demonstrating awareness of what the organisation as a whole is aiming to achieve (its vision), how each department and line of business is working towards that goal (business strategy) and where value is being created as a result.

Each business stakeholder will have their own flavour of how they are approaching these things – this is where the role becomes political, since there are balances and trade-offs that inevitably arise as a consequence. At the same time, the data leader needs to maintain integrity – that is, understanding when compromise is necessary and when it must be resisted because it could undermine foundational principles (e.g. data governance) or does not reflect what insights or analytics models are showing.

Data leadership is a classic example of where T-shaped skills are required: deep enough technical knowledge to oversee and direct the development of data resources, broad enough to encompass management of a department and its employees as well as engagement with other business leaders across the organisation, potentially right up to the top.

To be successful, the data leader also needs to demonstrate that they are continually improving the performance of the data department through building its skillset, productivity and engagement. That will mean having a clear development plan with staged investment requirements mapped against the business strategy of the organisation.

Understanding how to build personal credibility and integrity as a data leader using positive politics is a challenge that needs to be met and may involve the use of a self-assessment tool. Integrity equates to trust which is fundamental to engagement across the business. At times, this will require the most demanding of all leadership skills – saying no. Learning how and when to do this is not easy, but when done with integrity, it creates a very powerful and positive base in the business.

Alongside building integrity, the data leader will also need to build awareness of themselves as a political figure and also of the department as a strategic enabler. This will draw desirable projects towards the department, including Moon shot ideas that the line of business stakeholders imagined to be impossible – if the data leader demonstrates an appetite for big challenges, they will turn up!

——————— **DataIQ Way Marker** ———————

First, lead yourself

▼

Identifying your leadership style

Each data leader needs to find their own way of operating in the leadership space. One key to this is understanding the underlying personal motivations that have brought you to this position. Career Anchors are a useful tool which can identify the drivers you have and lead you towards the best approach to your own leadership. Table 6.1 shows the eight persistent anchors that inform the choices made by individuals.

Table 6.1: The eight Personal Anchors

Technical/ functional	These individuals enjoy being good at specific tasks and will work hard to become expert at them. They enjoy challenges and developing the skills to meet them, often relishing being better than others.
Managerial	These individuals thrive on responsibility and problem-solving – they want to be in charge of others and set them tasks. Emotional intelligence is an important asset.
Autonomy/ independence	Above all, these individuals want to work at their own pace without external interference. They are strong self-starters but can also find it hard to stick to common standards or processes.
Security/stability	These individuals want to be able to plan their careers, often becoming life-long employees in their organisations. Stability and risk-free work are important to them.
Entrepreneurial	Ownership and invention are hallmarks of these individuals. They want the financial rewards of their efforts and may pivot their career multiple times. They work well with teams who share their vision.
Service/ cause-oriented	Social impact or benefiting others are crucial to the motivation of these individuals, who will often set these outcomes above personal gain. Organisations and functions where this can be realised are more appealing, such as the public sector or HR.
Pure challenge	These individuals need the stimulus of the new, constantly looking for fresh tasks and challenges to take on. One consequence is that they have short job tenures as they may feel their incumbent work environment has become stagnant.
Lifestyle	Beyond work-life balance, the goal for these individuals is an integrated pattern of living. As part of this, they may take extended career breaks in order to pursue other interests, such as travelling. Equally, they may be driven by personal needs, such as caring for a family member or relative.

Among typical business managers who are on a career track towards seniority, the Managerial Career Anchor type is most evident. This may seem like an oxymoron given that managers need to have a preference for holding responsibility and task-setting.

What is important about this is the way in which human resources will lean towards candidates for management positions who demonstrate these qualities. Entrepreneurial types may also find favour if there is a start-up or disruptive dimension to the organisation.

Among data leaders, however, the more dominant Career Anchors tend to be:

- *Technical/functional* – data practitioners are eager to develop their technical skills and prove their abilities.

- *Autonomy* – data practitioners often want to sit and work on a problem on their own until they have cracked it.

- *Service/cause-oriented* – data practitioners can be driven by a desire to use data for good, especially if they are working in the public sector or not-for-profit.

- *Lifestyle* – this has also begun to emerge as a Career Anchor among data practitioners, not least because of the influence of the start-up/digital disruptor culture that offers a very different style of working practice.

As a result, there is a tension between what an organisation's HR department may view as the right profile and career development for managerial or leadership roles within the data department. This can lead to disappointment on both sides – for HR when a chosen candidate struggles or performs differently from what was expected and from the data leader seeking to advance who finds themself uncomfortable or unsuited to the leadership role.

By recognising your own Career Anchors and understanding the expected model of leadership you may encounter, you can improve your chances of advancement and define what additional skills or capabilities you may need to develop.

Deliver

━━━━━ DataIQ Way Marker ━━━━━

Take the lead on value

▼

Prioritising data projects by value

BAU demands for data support are a constant. Delivering solely against BAU is not a sustainable value proposition for the data department, however. Firstly, it creates a false expectation among stakeholders that any project they can think of will be adopted and delivered. Secondly, data practitioners will find themselves struggling to keep up with a blur of projects that have overlapping and competing deadlines. Thirdly, the data department will never manage to progress and rise up the maturity curve to become proactive.

In order to address this challenge, the data leader needs to adopt a number of approaches that will begin to channel the demand tsunami, apply proper controls and prepare data for its next evolution. It is only by looking beyond BAU towards more transformational projects that real value creation can be pursued.

In the early stages of the maturity of data, demand will outstrip supply, especially before automation, standardisation and self-service tools are introduced. While data leaders are always tempted to respond positively, even if it means the department operating over capacity, this is not sustainable in the long term. A system of scoring projects needs to be developed in partnership with stakeholders which allows the workstream to be properly ordered.

Key dimensions of the scoring system include:

- business deadline

- business impact

- data resourcing required

- timeline.

In this way, the briefing and prioritisation process becomes a properly managed, business-like negotiation where both parties understand and have visibility of what is being agreed. Collaboration tools can be deployed at this point to ensure there is visibility of the workstream and the priorities which are ahead of any new project in the queue.

During this negotiation, value attribution also needs to be agreed (see Chapter 9 for more detail on how to do this). If metrics and recognition for data's input to a project are in place at the outset, then the data leader is well placed to demonstrate the ongoing value creation being delivered by the department.

Measuring productivity in the data realm

While much of the focus around data projects tends to be on achieving cost efficiencies within business processes, such as through enhancing productivity using automation, data leaders also need to keep a close eye on the productivity of their own department. As with the need for prioritisation outlined earlier, there are performance metrics that need to be put in place to help justify the continued investment made by the organisation into this area.

Simple measures, such as task completion, offer a top-line indicator of productivity. If combined with measures of stakeholder satisfaction, this may be sufficient to show that the data department is working effectively. But it also seems like a limited way for the department to measure itself given its own vision of being the provider of the evidence base for the business.

The standard measure of productivity is total output divided by total input. At the top level, this would equate to the total business benefit delivered by the data department divided by its overheads. Assuming the data leader has visibility of the running costs of the department, it is possible to keep a running total of those benefits, but such metrics do not just happen – they need to be real, clearly defined, ideally repeatable, visible in data sets, agreed by key stakeholders and finance, and preferably associated with rewards or sanctions if they are/are not met.

Among the most advanced users of data, a benefits realisation manager may be embedded in the department to enable it to demonstrate financial benefits to a standard acceptable to finance. While this may not be an option for all, it does demonstrate that this degree of specificity and accuracy is possible.

Given the mixed nature of the demands on the department, from BAU to innovation, it is important to try to maintain a balanced portfolio of projects, with a blend of metrics with both short-term and long-term outcomes in view. Some of these will deliver significantly in excess of costs and with potentially low levels of input, while others may be net negative (yet still desirable for the organisation).

It is also the case that capacity is limited compared to demand. By rigorously exploring metrics, the data department can start to show the value it has discovered against the value delivered and thereby show its productivity. When attaching metrics to projects, attention should therefore be paid to deliverability against these potential options:

- *Hard cash measures (project-based)* – every project picked up by the data department should ideally have a specific cash benefit attached. While this may be relatively easy to identify, such as a reduction in marketing spend through optimisation of targeting, or an increase in sales conversion through website improvements, the harder aspect is getting agreement from the business stakeholder to acknowledge the role of data in delivering this improvement. Time management and measurement, like that practised by consultants, may be required to identify the true level of productivity.

- *Hard cash measures (company-level)* – measuring this may be a two-step process, i.e. converting a reduction in headcount into pounds saved for the business. Where the impact is at a corporate level, it can be harder to draw a direct line between the inputs from data and the eventual cash benefits, so reaching agreement at the outset on how this will be accounted for is essential.

- *Soft measures* – some of the goals for data projects will be softer in nature with no direct financial benefit, such as looking to improve employee satisfaction or customer NPS as a result of new, improved processes. These clearly have multiple inputs and rely on processes being executed according to the recommendations from the data department, but should be accounted for proportionally. In regulated industries, such as financial services, organisations specifically have to demonstrate soft benefits for customers, such as through 'Treating Customers Fairly' rules or showing transactional NPS. Productivity by the data department may also be measured on soft measures, such as stakeholder satisfaction, in a similar way.

- *Recognised, attributable measures* – given the complexity of what data may recommend and the multiple elements involved in making it operational, drawing a direct line to financial or even soft measures may be hard or impossible. One way to step around this obstacle is to agree with stakeholders from the outset a percentage of any incremental gains or cost savings that will be attributed to the input from this function. Even though it may not seem scientific, it is better to accept an estimated figure than to fail to agree and miss out on the eventual benefit being seen as stemming from data science.

While these metrics provide departmental-level indicators of productivity, the data leader will also need to measure individual-level output. A growing method for this aligns with the adoption of agile as the working practice within the data department. Within this approach, each project is broken down into a set of user stories and these are assigned points based on their complexity. During each sprint, the team will be capable of tackling a set number of points, determined by the scrum master – this is sometimes referred to as velocity. At both team level and individual level, the total points delivered during each sprint can be tracked, providing a measure of productivity.

Managing for productivity

As discussed elsewhere in this book, knowledge work has important differences from standard types of employment and data differs again from typical knowledge work. Yet there are important findings from modern management practices that can be deployed in the knowledge department. One of these is recognising and using the levers available to maintain and enhance individual productivity.

It is an easily observable fact that data practitioners can be highly committed and deeply engaged with a project or appear detached and unenthusiastic – there is often little middle ground. Creating the right conditions to gain commitment is therefore an important task for the data leader who wants to optimise the productivity of the data department.

A meta-study of academic research carried out by the Centre for Evidence-Based Management (cebma.org) identified six factors that most impact on knowledge work productivity, and are therefore likely to be highly present among data practitioners. As Figure 6.1 shows, these strongly correlate with creating a data culture, demonstrating leadership and putting key enablers in place.

Figure 6.1: The six factors of knowledge worker productivity

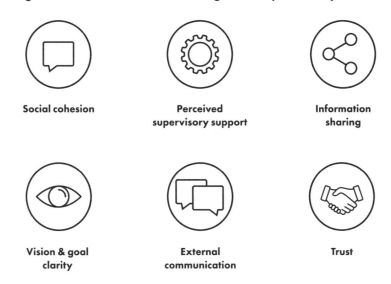

| Social cohesion | Perceived supervisory support | Information sharing |
| Vision & goal clarity | External communication | Trust |

Source: Centre for Evidence-Based Management - CEBMa

The study also identified weightings for five of these factors which had the largest effect (see Table 6.2). Surprisingly, external communication was not found to influence knowledge worker productivity, perhaps because this usually takes place after tasks have been completed and is therefore extrinsic to the work, rather than being intrinsic.

Table 6.2: Knowledge worker productivity factors

Rank	Factor	Weighting
1	Social cohesion	0.5–0.7
2	Perceived supervisory support	0.5
3	Information sharing	0.5
4	Vision/goal clarity	0.5
5	Trust	0.3–0.6

Source: Centre for Evidence-Based Management – CEBMa

As this analysis clearly indicates, there is huge potential for the data leader to have a positive impact on the productivity of the data department (or indeed the opposite effect), depending on their approach. The factors identified by CEBMa are exactly those which the DataIQ Way has been architected to support and develop, providing thereby a framework for a data leader to enhance and progress the impact and performance of their teams and department.

Measuring productivity

---------------------- **DataIQ Way Marker** ----------------------
Even knowledge workers need to be measured
▼

Productivity is an abiding concern for business leaders, economists and governments alike. Achieving higher levels of productivity is one way to increase the wealth of a nation or the value of a business. It is also a major part of the appeal of data in its 'fourth industrial revolution' role, since the deployment of automation, AI and ML are all intended to enhance the output of humans or allow for levels of activity which humans could never achieve. From the dark warehouses that fulfil e-commerce orders to the robotic planting and harvesting of farmers' fields, productivity gains are strongly anticipated.

So how does a data leader set about measuring (and optimising) the productivity of data teams and individuals? It is an issue that has been barely thought about in many departments – monitoring project requests against delivery and backlog is the bare metric typically in use.

Better is required, yet there are limited models to adopt for this. Two aspects of knowledge work and data work in particular also need to be accepted. Firstly, what may appear unproductive may be a necessary part of the task – just as staring out of a window may lead to the spark of inspiration required, so reading academic articles may lead to a data scientist connecting two previously disparate concepts. Secondly, there is a lot of grunt work involved in data that is neither value-generating nor directly productive. Simply assembling the data required for a project typically involves 50% to 80% of an analyst's time. Until this has been automated, it is unavoidable and needs to be built into productivity metrics. Similarly, most knowledge workers spend more time in meetings or doing administrative work – up to two-thirds of their time according to a 2013 article in *Harvard Business Review* ('Making Time for the Work That Matters' by Julian Birkinshaw and Jordan Cohen) – than directly on origination.

Agile has offered one method that has started to be adopted, which involves assigning points to each project and then measuring how long it takes for each data practitioner to complete that task, then cumulatively tracking their points haul over a period to average out the different levels of difficulty involved. Data leaders can develop a benchmark for their teams and individuals within a relatively short period of time against which each can be tracked. Rewards or mitigation are then applied if productivity exceeds the benchmark or falls short.

This points-based system also avoids the major pitfall of standard productivity metrics in the data arena. Conventionally, productivity is measured as output divided by input, where input is usually hours worked. As any data leader will know, the pace of activity across the department is constantly flexing with some elements of any project moving slowly before a rapid acceleration towards a key point.

Similarly, there are interdependencies and nuances in how individuals work that can be highly complex and difficult to measure, often tied to the nature of the role they are in. For example, a team member may not produce a lot of direct output on their own, but the rest of the team is highly dependent on what they do. This is likely to be true of data quality and data governance roles, for example. These individuals are 'force multipliers' since their actions help to enhance what other team members are able to achieve. A data scientist may be heavily reliant on a data engineer to deliver a working model into the production environment – their individual outputs are very different, but mutually dependent.

For this reason, measuring productivity at a team (or squad) level may be more appropriate and effective. It also allows for culture to play a key role in ensuring the right working environment where support, recognition, communication and reward all keep individuals engaged and active. The agile concept of velocity – the number of tasks a team is capable of achieving within a given two-week sprint – is useful to this end. But a careful eye open needs to be maintained by the data leader for issues that can suddenly degrade this capability, especially if these are external to the data department, such as IT downtime or all-hands company meetings.

Grow

─────── **DataIQ Way Marker** ───────

Don't stand still because data doesn't

▼

How to maintain momentum for data and analytics

Momentum is an important aspect of the task facing any data leader as they develop this department in their organisation. In year one, data benefits from the excitement of being the latest new thing, as well as the opportunities afforded by low-hanging fruit. In year two, working practices become embedded, which should lead to more efficient ways of working, but can also codify unresolved issues.

However, by year three, if the data office has been slow in building data literacy across the enterprise or in bringing significant benefits and transformation, it can face deep challenges from the business, even the prospect of being broken up or downsized. While this may not be the fault of the department – the organisation may have been resistant to change, for example – it is nonetheless an easy target that often lacks political cover.

Maturity is therefore one of the key indicators of momentum which needs to be constantly measured and demonstrated. Unless the organisation is making incremental steps up the maturity curve, it may start to believe that data itself is at fault as a practice, rather than other process or cultural issues.

At the same time, data leaders need to be aware of another facet which is outside of their control – shareholder value. Although data is constantly seeking to draw a straight line between its activities and the company P&L (see Chapter 9), two of the biggest pressures on the C-suite are share price and investor sentiment.

When a CEO does get replaced, it usually heralds considerable disruption and reorganisation, not least because the incoming CEO will want to put their stamp on the business (and often as not flush out anything they consider not to have worked or to be tainted by association with their predecessor). This has been witnessed directly by multiple DataIQ Leaders members in the retail, insurance and logistics sectors.

Job tenure for CDOs is a little harder to calculate robustly since there is a much smaller cohort with a shorter job history than across the C-suite generally. But among the 28 individuals holding this job title in the DataIQ 100 list of 2019, 12 had changed companies in the 12 previous months – 43% of the group. It also appears that female CDOs are more loyal – while they represent 46% of the group, only 38% switched organisations, below the overall average.

So the CDO may well find themself to be the incumbent expert in transformational data opportunities for the organisation when a new CEO arrives. This can be a strong basis on which to push for growth, arguing for additional investment to drive leading-edge projects such as AI, ML and automation.

But this does require careful political handling to position data as the enabler, rather than the legacy of a failed previous business leader. Momentum can act in two competing ways – as a forward force or as resistance.

The business world has experienced multiple hype cycles around data and analytics, especially since the explosion of interest in big data as a theme from 2012 onwards. The main cycle of the current decade is defined by AI and ML. The challenge for data leaders is to use these waves of hype to pull along foundational projects or to close out activities that have been lagging behind.

Additionally, it is vital to associate these core data tasks with new strategies such as business transformations that get launched by the CEO. If data can get written into strategy, policy, values and more, then it is that much harder to separate out and downgrade. This does not mitigate the risk from competing divisional CEOs with non-aligned views on what purpose data should have. But those are perennial political problems that will exist across the organisation and are not unique to data.

As long as the data leader knows how to tell a good story and is convincing, there is every chance of keeping things moving in the right direction.

Talent management and recruitment

If the data department is to grow, it will need additional human resources. In most territories, demand continues to outstrip supply for individuals with the right skills, experience and appetite. A particular recruitment challenge for legacy organisations is the need to compete as exciting places to work against digital platforms and start-ups. Internal branding can play a part – at the insurance provider Aviva, its global data and analytics practice has been branded Quantum to distinguish it from the corporate organisation and culture. Even the physical appearance of its offices is markedly different from the main headquarters to reinforce this (and is in part why it has won the DataIQ Award for Best Place to Work in Data two years in a row).

There is an upside for legacy organisations in their ability to allow graduates to work on both digital systems and data at scale, something start-ups are unable to offer. Also, data teams in legacy organisations have more opportunities to make an impact than within global digital platforms, where the focus is more often on optimisation of specific, existing processes than on identifying new opportunities and breakthroughs.

It is also the case that not every graduate wants to work in those global or start-up environments. At one law firm, part of its pitch to recruit PhDs has been the challenge of transforming the huge amounts of data it holds on dispute resolution in paper and electronic documents into codified and machine-readable data sets that can be used to automate processes.

Major organisations tend to have well-established graduate programmes. Recently, some of these have adapted to new skills requirements in the data department, such as the data science graduate scheme at a global bank which is now in its second year and offers a combination of experience across customer science, ML and data engineering. The bank still runs its broader graduate programme which sees selected candidates rotate through credit, lending, operations, engineering and also data and analytics. Notably, the CDO at the bank said the mix of skills and profiles across this scheme was welcome for its impact on diversity and inclusion.

Elsewhere, an international media organisation has needed to educate its HR colleagues to understand that classic graduate recruitment does not yield the right candidates for a global data team. The former mindset saw data as a subset of IT which could be fed from the same stream of human capital. Shifting these attitudes and approaches can take time, however. In several instances, getting the right talent acquisition in place for data and analytics has taken two years.

One common problem has been how to deal with the volume of applications that are made – it is not unusual to receive several hundred CVs for each open position. A global facilities management company is working with a specialist recruitment platform which manages this via an AI-driven pre-interview solution that provides feedback on each candidate compared to the available role in order to filter the funnel down to manageable levels.

For more senior roles, attracting talent becomes a more complex balance of the transactional (pay and benefits), professional (task complexity and variety) and personal (Career Anchors and lifestyle). No single organisation has a monopoly on all three because there are diverse reasons why established data leaders decide to move on. Often, it is the personal brand of the data leader which can make the difference – great practitioners want to work with other great practitioners. Being visible and recognised across the data industry is therefore an important aspect of growing as a data leader.

———— DataIQ Way Marker ————

Lead like a boss

Heading for the C-suite

The CDO experienced significant growth as a role in the 2010s as ever more organisations created a data office and appointed a CDO at its head. In 2017, Gartner predicted that by the end of 2019, 90% of organisations would have appointed a CDO. At first, regulated industries had to respond to new legislation that required better control and visibility of their data asset in the wake of the financial crash of 2008–10.

But even a casual survey of UK plcs will reveal that this Gartner forecast has proven to be way off, potentially by a factor of ten. Neither is the number of post-holders the only problem with this position. Use of the word 'chief' to describe the role has given a false expectation about the seniority of the individuals in it. At last count, only two companies in the UK FTSE 100 had a CDO sitting on the board. Everywhere else, this position tends to be a direct report to another CxO (who is often part of the extended executive board, but not the board-level executive itself). Typically, this is the chief financial officer, chief technology officer or in some cases, the chief marketing officer.

This is understandable in those regulated organisations given the nature of the activity for which they needed a senior data leader. Often described as CDO v1.0, the focus was mainly on data protection and compliance, ensuring the data asset was only used within legal parameters. This type of CDO operates within the technology department or as part of the compliance team and has no direct line to value creation – this takes place inside advanced analytics or data science functions that operate within a host department. It is also the case that a data practitioner drawn to this type of CDO role is unlikely ever to be promoted to a board-level position.

More recently, CDO v2.0 has started to emerge as a leadership position with stand-alone authority and responsibility for the data department, including analytics. Yet many of these CDOs still have no place on the board. In discussions with data leaders, DataIQ has identified that the path to a top-level seat is currently being crowded by chief information officers or chief digital officers, both having authority over the CDO. One driver of this is the importance of digital transformation, which is viewed as primarily a technology-led change, rather than a fundamental change to processes and a mindset that is rooted in data.

But the approach and attitude of data leaders themselves also play a major role in keeping the CDO off the board. In a discussion during 2020 with members of DataIQ Leaders, it became clear that data is not necessarily seen as a career track leading to senior management. While data leaders may want personal status and recognition, plus investment and support for their function, this does not translate into a relentless pursuit of promotion. In fact, most see this as undesirable because it will take them too far away from the day-to-day practice of data, which is their real motivation.

Career Anchors are part of this disposition, as discussed earlier in this chapter, leading to a cohort of data leaders whose primary focus is on how data can impact on the business, rather than on how the business can become a true data native. Yet for this ideal state to be approached, the board needs to have the voice of data clearly represented.

In the long term, this is likely to arise out of a new generation of business leaders who instinctively expect to pursue evidence-based decision-making. But in the short term, it creates a skills and leadership gap which risks other parties, whose vision has a different set of roots, taking advantage.

DATA LITERACY STEPCOUNTER

Leadership for the CDO involves managing upwards and downwards to ensure continual growth and clear productivity.

The CDO needs to step outside their technical skillset and become an effective leader.

Steps 19–22:

19. Understand the nature of leading a data department and the motivations that drive your team.

20. Focus on the productivity of your department and measuring its output and value.

21. Recognise your Career Anchors and what suits your style of leadership.

22. Decide whether you want to join the senior executive or stay in the data lane.

CHAPTER 7
Data teams

Roadmap – in this chapter:

- Photobox tackled performance and retention issues by creating a data squad.

- Guilds, squads and tribes create an agile, working structure but can be challenging for stakeholders, leaders and practitioners.

- Communication is critical both within teams and between teams and stakeholders.

- Principles exist that make data storytelling and data visualisation more effective.

- Creating a data brand gives the data team better visibility and engagement levels.

- Automating routine tasks frees data teams to tackle higher value projects. Democratisation of data has a similar benefit.

- Data teams need to constantly scan the horizon for the next opportunity, technique or technology.

Collaborate

———— DataIQ Way Marker ————

Work in agile, behave in squads

▼

Photobox builds a data squad

As the song says, "things can only get better". When you are experiencing an annual rate of staff attrition running at more than 45%, low morale among remaining data practitioners and a blame culture each time problems arise, you know something has to change. That was the situation facing Photobox in 2019 when Andy Ruckley arrived as director of data, BI and analytics. Data was operating in three silos – data engineers, BI developers and insight analysts – with independent working practices and projects being remotely handed off.

"We needed a watershed moment that brought all the teams together, unify against a set of issues, and get to an outcome where we could focus on a higher mission and their role in delivering it," said Ruckley. His solution was to create the data squad as a transformational way of working to leverage the value in the existing capability and the skills incumbent practitioners had.

To kick-start this new approach, he held an offsite meeting to clear the air about all of the issues and identify common problems. It quickly emerged that all three teams were struggling with the decade-old legacy data platform that lacked data management principles and documentation. Duplication of effort was also recognised, together with a lack of communication.

While fixing the technology would help, it would take time and would not be a magic bullet. Instead, the concept of working as a squad, respecting the expertise across all teams and focusing on making the business more data-driven achieved buy-in. This cohered around the vision statement, "Making Photobox smarter for improved decision-making". This shifted the focus away from data infrastructure and processes and onto outcomes.

For each of the three teams within the squad, their specific area of value creation could also be identified: data engineers ensuring data availability for critical business decisions; BI developers eliminating manual report creation and delivering key reports on time (which also reduced data processing load compared to identical reports previously being run ten times per hour); insight analysts diving deeper into data to ask more complex questions.

Another key out-take from the meeting was the data squad recognising how important it was for the data department to support insight analysts, who work embedded alongside business stakeholders. To support this, a new data squad fortnightly newsletter was launched which highlights new insights, definitions of key business concepts and any data quality issues. A monthly mini-hackathon has helped to deepen the sense of shared effort and maintain focus on the migration to the new data platform, ensuring data engineers and insight analysts alike share needs and business perspectives.

A significant impact from the creation of the data squad has been an increase in employee engagement and a reduction in attrition to below 10% as at June 2020.

Guilds, squads and tribes

While the data department may appear to be a singular entity when being established, it does not always operate in this way. Elements of its activities may sit separately within lines of business, such as data engineering being part of IT, or as stand-alone functions, such as advanced analytics or data science. According to DataIQ research, while 34.5% of organisations have a centralised data department, the same percentage have federated data while 13.8% operate on a hub-and-spoke basis. That means nearly half of data teams (48.3%) could find themselves working alongside stakeholders rather than their own peers. Data science operates in a more consolidated way with 40.7% having a centralised function and 26.7% a team working within a centralised analytics function (see Figure 7.1).

Figure 7.1: How is data science set up in your organisation?

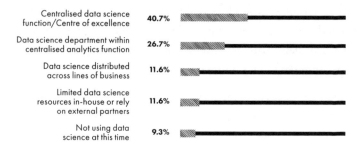

Centralised data science function/Centre of excellence — 40.7%

Data science department within centralised analytics function — 26.7%

Data science distributed across lines of business — 11.6%

Limited data science resources in-house or rely on external partners — 11.6%

Not using data science at this time — 9.3%

Whatever approach has been taken to the data department and its component functions, the data leader is presented with a critical challenge – how to ensure teams are collaborating effectively, sharing their knowledge, maintaining productivity and delivering to stakeholders. Agile has been widely adopted as a working practice to address this. But while agile describes how to approach and manage fast-moving challenges, there is also a need for a people management structure that reflects this new way of working.

Squads and tribes have emerged as a loose matrix solution that both supports agile analytics and also the socialised, non-hierarchical mindset of younger workers. Originated within Spotify in 2012 as part of its adoption of agile for engineering solutions, the concept has its origins in lean manufacturing and Kanban approaches to continuous improvement. It is a specifically people management tool for organising practitioners and helping them to maintain a sense of ownership, identity and belonging, which can be hard to achieve given the rapid turnover of projects within agile working.

For any data department, the creation of communities of practice, guilds, squads and tribes should be a fundamental part of its operating model. Rather, for any data department above a certain size, it is essential because squads and tribes are a matter of scale. The anthropologist Robin Dunbar posited that the number of social relationships which any individual can sustain is between 100 and 250, with a typical average of 150. Studies of social groups repeatedly find evidence of this, leading to Dunbar's Number being recognised as a constant.

In the same way, data departments need to have reached a certain scale before the concept of squads and tribes becomes relevant and viable. This is a consequence of the internal logic of the approach itself and also of human nature. A small unit of, say, 10 to 30 practitioners will be able to operate in a stable, self-organising way without any formal overlay. Similarly, the mathematics of squads and tribes demands a minimum of around 20 practitioners in order to be meaningful (see Figure 7.2). With an agile team only meant to include ten people, there is little point formalising this structure if the entire data department is only two or three times that size – everybody will pretty much know what everybody else is doing already.

Figure 7.2: Squads and tribes model

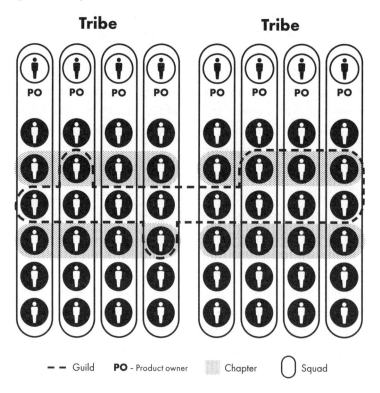

Defining the structure

While the concept of squads and tribes has a fixed meaning, the definitions of what they do will vary by organisation. This is best set out through a process of discovery and mapping, such as that carried out by a national grocery chain. After the data leader learned about this working practice and decided to adopt it, they spent time in workshops identifying all of the activities which the data department was carrying out.

These were then grouped logically as product areas under a product owner. Each of these products is a tribe involving practitioners from across the department who routinely carry out the same tasks, for example building data models, segmenting customers, defining KPIs, etc. Tribes are usually limited to under 100 members.

To respond to specific projects required by stakeholders, multi-disciplinary teams are needed – these are the squads. Each of these faces off to a specific stakeholder in the business and is typically made up of between three and eight practitioners. Squads can be self-selecting under the supervision of a scrum master to ensure balance and fairness. At the completion of each project, the squad breaks up and returns to its tribe.

Communities of practice are supra-tribal groups who share an interest, skillset or desire to learn, for example specific coding languages or analytics techniques. Some organisations have both chapters – groups of specialists with common responsibilities – and guilds – informal groups with common interests – although this is generally the preserve of very large-scale data departments.

Adopting this approach is generally done by data leaders because of the way it mirrors the agile sprint cycle, creates cross-functional working and knowledge sharing, while avoiding fixed-size teams which lack the ability to flex their resources according to demand.

Practitioners can welcome this model because it is based on trust, rather than command and control. In large departments, it creates connections at multiple levels while also maintaining a sense of identity. Exposure to new and different projects keeps practitioners interested and engaged.

This approach is not the same as an organisational chart and is not about the specific roles involved. As a consequence, it can seem too loose for hierarchical organisations and can be confusing given the multiple memberships which any one individual can have (squad, tribe, community of practice or guild).

For data leaders, the move to adopt squads and tribes can prove difficult to make if they are used to a conventional structure. Stakeholders may also be concerned by the loss of a permanent relationship with specific practitioners, since squad members are likely to vary over time. Autonomy for practitioners can also seem excessive if it extends to how all resources and time are allocated. Diversity may also be hard to impose in a system of self-selection.

DataIQ Way Marker

Data must be seen to be believed

Building external relationships

External communication is one of the six key dimensions of productivity for knowledge workers, as we saw in Chapter 6. While it may not carry the same weight as the other five, it is still fundamental when it comes to linking investment in the data department to value creation for the organisation. Data can appear to its internal customers as something of a 'black box', especially the work of functions like analytics and data science which generate models through an invisible, quasi-magical process.

The level of communication with stakeholders has a significant impact on this, especially if data teams learn the language of the business and thereby reduce the knowledge gap between counter-parties. This further underlines why building data literacy across the organisation is an important goal for the data leader.

Communication within data teams and between teams and the data leader is also essential. This is best achieved through a combination of formal meetings where information is exchanged in a structured way and by creating an informal culture which encourages casual interactions. The physical set-up and appearance of the data workplace can help to enable this – many mature data departments have adopted the look and feel of digital start-ups to encourage this unstructured interaction.

For data leaders in particular, a further step is essential – making the link between what the data teams have done and successful business outcomes. It is often assumed that simply doing good work will lead to recognition by internal customers. But this is very rarely the case – those stakeholders need to be constantly informed, educated and reminded of how central data is to the success of their own line of business.

Federating data teams into the business or working in a hub-and-spoke model may seem the obvious way to ensure these relationships are built. But they are not the only way for this to happen. If stakeholders are using agile themselves, then the opportunity exists to introduce data teams into project squads as part of the essential multi-disciplinary mix involved.

Above all, data needs to be visible to other departments across the organisation, rather than keeping to itself as a backroom operation. Data teams should be encouraged to engage with activities within the business, not just within the data department, to support this goal.

DataIQ Way Marker

Information flows better across weak bridges

The strength of weak ties

One compelling reason for encouraging data teams to interact beyond their direct peer group – indeed, beyond their comfort zone – is the strength of weak ties. This sociological concept was first put forward in 1973 by Mark S. Granovetter at Johns Hopkins University. He identified that most studies of social networks had looked at the strength of ties within formal groups at a micro-level. This is still the main area of attention when using social network analysis, for example.

Granovetter's insight was that such analyses could show if a social group – such as a data team – was strongly engaged within itself, but they do not relate that team strength to a macro-level pattern, such as whether the organisation is becoming more data literate and building a data culture as a result of its interactions with data teams.

The reason for this is that strong ties within a group or between individuals act as a block to information flowing between those groups and individuals who are indirectly connected on one side to groups and individuals who are indirectly connected on the other side.

In practice, this might mean a strong tie exists between the customer analytics team and the data governance function, for example. But the marketing team which the customer analytics team supports is unlikely to have a strong direct link to the data governance function – as a consequence, information about data governance issues is unlikely to flow to that marketing team. This is because "no strong tie is a bridge", as Granovetter puts it. The data governance team will communicate clearly and directly to customer analytics. It might even assume that those messages get passed onto marketing. In reality, this does not happen.

But when data teams are encouraged to build weak ties beyond the data department, for example through external communications or involvement in social activities run by the business, it creates a network of connections that allow information to be diffused more widely and more rapidly. This is because it takes less time and commitment to build weak ties, which therefore takes up less time for all parties involved and are non-exclusive, allowing for many more weak ties to be built than strong ties. So if the leader of the marketing team needs to find out about an aspect of data governance, for example, they can tap up their customer analytics contact for an introduction more easily than if they try to contact the data governance team directly.

This effect can be recognised in the way brands use social media influencers to disseminate product information, positive reviews or aspirational images. The networks built by those influencers are based on weak ties that take little time and effort to create – a simple follow, like or share – and benefit from the multiplier effect whereby immediate contacts bring their own contacts into the network. There is also little social cost involved in disseminating brand stories across weak ties, whereas sharing information with a strongly bonded contact carries a high personal cost-benefit.

Data leaders should therefore pay attention to the extent of their data team's weak ties because of the impact this has on the diffusion of information. According to the research, any damage to a weak tie will on average be more harmful to the probability of information being transmitted than if a strong tie is removed. As a driver of data literacy and building data culture, the more widely data teams have casual interaction with the business, the more likely the organisation is to absorb core concepts and behaviours.

Communicate

──────────── **DataIQ Way Marker** ────────────

Show the destination, not the journey

▼

How data storytelling and data visualisation work

It is easy to view soft skills as being the preserve of the humanities and of little use to the sciences. That is true only if the audience for what scientists produce is only other scientists and then only if they specialise in the same domain. For data scientists – indeed, for all analysts and everybody working in data – the audience will most often be non-technical, business-oriented. These stakeholders may be highly numerate, as in the case of financial directors and CFOs, or highly visual, such as brand marketers and CMOs. But all of them will be consumers of data outputs to some degree.

The existence of a Professor for the Public Understanding of Science at New College, Oxford – a post currently held by Marcus du Sautoy – is proof enough that translating complex concepts into accessible language is now a mainstream issue. It is also important to use communication skills to help to demystify data and analytics, thereby reducing the risk of becoming seen as a black box operation that nobody in the business understands and therefore does not trust.

Data leaders also need to acknowledge that much of what happens within the data department is not done within some inaccessible sphere of coding or statistics. As du Sautoy himself has said: "Many of the best algorithms contain no numbers or equations at all, but are full of mathematical thinking. And it is those algorithms that are creating efficient approaches to a whole range of business solutions, from the distribution of goods from supermarket warehouses to decisions about flight schedules at Heathrow airport." Similarly, data practitioners need to recognise that their business stakeholders, especially senior leaders, have little interest in the processes and techniques used by the data department to reach an insight or create a model. What they want is the basis for a decision, whether that is a key report, predictive model or business opportunity.

Data storytelling and data visualisation therefore need to become a core part of the toolkit of practitioners within the data department if they are to gain traction externally. At a simple level, it is evident that plotting data makes it easier to identify patterns or structures that would not be revealed by the rows of a spreadsheet. This was recognised as long ago as 1786 by William Playfair who pioneered the use of graphs to explore data.

A number of foundational works have subsequently codified the effectiveness of different approaches to the way data is visualised. In 1983, Edward Tufte published his book *The Visual Display of Quantitative Information*, a landmark in the realm of data visualisation which has informed practitioners in the four decades since. In 1984, William S. Cleveland and Robert McGill published the findings of their experiments into the relative strengths and weaknesses of different types of chart when visualising data in their paper, *Graphical Perception: Theory, Experimentation, and Application to the Development of Graphical Methods* (http://faculty.washington. edu/aragon/classes/hcde511/s12/readings/cleveland84.pdf).

In 2010, Jeffrey Heer and Michael Bostock re-examined those findings in the light of the emergence of digital channels in their paper, *Crowdsourcing Graphical Perception: Using Mechanical Turk to Assess Visualisation Design* (https://idl.cs.washington.edu/files/2010-MTurk-CHI.pdf). They found that the same principles identified by Tufte, and Cleveland and McGill in the 1980s were still true in the digital era. Figure 7.3 shows the comparative effectiveness of different data visualisations based on these two studies.

Figure 7.3: Comparative effectiveness of data visualisations

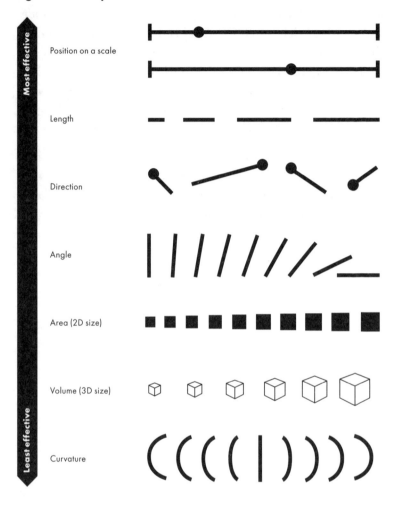

Data storytelling is arguably the junior discipline – humans developed the written word after visual imagery. But it is just as essential since it brings into play a key dimension that is familiar to technical and non-technical audiences alike – that of narrative. While a great data visualisation makes complex data instantly accessible, it still needs to be explained, the context provided, caveats given and inferences drawn.

To do this, data practitioners can draw on the skills they already use in everyday conversation, but amplified and made specific to the task. Using scenarios will make forecasting models come alive for decision-makers, for example, while metaphors position difficult concepts into everyday realities. Emotions can also be used to make a data story compelling by drawing on the classical constructs of Ethos, Logos and Pathos. While everybody is familiar with the use of these techniques in drama, applying them into everyday practice needs to be trained.

If data visualisation is the set design and data storytelling is the script, then presentation skills are the acting required to inhabit the former and bring the latter to life. That does not mean data practitioners need to aspire to be actors, rather there are skills drawn on in that profession which are just transferrable.

At its heart, this means finding a style or persona that enables you to present to a room full of peers or seniors – sometimes friendly, perhaps hostile or disengaged – with confidence and authority. Perhaps most importantly, it involves recognising that fear is a natural response to this situation, but can be harnessed as an energy. Good presenters can make even difficult news acceptable and complex insights digestible, winning belief and support even when what they have to say does not want to be heard.

As Tom Spencer, head of customer data science at Aviva, says: "Keep communication clear and concise. In a technical field, it's all too tempting to fall into jargon and complexity. Senior execs are extremely busy and bombarded with information all day – make it easy for them to understand your message."

Building a data brand

A key aspect of increasing the maturity of the organisation's adoption and usage of data, especially when trying to reach the level of data literate or data cultured, is to move beyond the perception of data as a tool that is simply applied to a predefined task. If lines of business develop their strategies first and then look for the data to support it, they will be permanently stuck in a low level of adoption that is sub-optimal.

Anita Fernqvist, CDO and director of operations at Zurich Insurance UK, has recognised this challenge: "Investing the time to ensure that data and analytics is at the table when it comes to business strategy debates is critical. It allows for early identification of opportunities to innovate and ensuring that we are part of the solution and not simply order-takers.

"In my view, this is a two-way commitment – as data professionals we need to be out there listening, challenging, responding and providing proactive support, while market-facing functions need to work with us to engender a true passion and understanding for their part of the business, their customer challenges and strategic priorities so that we can all work as one team. An engaged and passionate data team knows no bounds. So the ask would be across any industry to invite them to the party!"

Data teams can bring about change by engaging with stakeholders, finding data champions and building a data brand. This may become literally a brand, such as Aviva's Quantum, or it may be a more behavioural identification. Samsung Europe took this approach when its European Consumer and Market Insight (CMI) team and the digital leadership joined forces to deliver a transformation across the business. Aligned with the slogan, #DoWhatYouCant, new values and ways of working were adopted alongside a unified data infrastructure and consolidated BI tools and budgets. The new slogan and ways of working helped to develop a new culture based around the core values of people, excellence, change, integrity and co-prosperity. Using lean processes, agile methodology and collaborative tools, the team was able to maintain the quality of its work, even throughout the disruption of the Covid-19 pandemic.

There are a number of benefits from building a data brand. These include:

- *Visibility* – stakeholders in the business know where to come for support or who to involve from the data department in their projects.

- *Recognition* – if a major challenge faced by data is to have its value creation properly recognised, then having a brand makes it more likely that stakeholders will be willing to attribute impact.

- *Opportunity* – it is more likely that innovation will be identified with data if it is constantly demonstrating its successes and putting on roadshows to explain the art of the possible.

This last area of activity should not be underestimated and is another key area where communication skills can be highly effective. In fact, it has even led to the creation of an entirely new role within data departments, that of the data journalist. Depending on the nature of the organisation, it may be appropriate to employ an individual whose specific job is to discover, translate and explain to the wider organisation what the data team has been doing (or is capable of).

Innovate

—————————— **DataIQ Way Marker** ——————————
Feed the mind, automate the body

▼

The drive to automate business as usual

Data teams demand diversity, not just in terms of the make-up of the team but also with regard to the tasks they are asked to undertake. Repetitive, low-value activities, such as reporting or data extraction, may be central to all data-driven processes. But they also consume energy and attention that could be better applied to innovative and value-creating projects.

To avoid falling into the trap of being a reactive BAU machine, the data department needs to become a literal machine where possible – applying robotic process automation to routine tasks, developing ML to carry out the heavy lifting. The business case for this is significant. According to research by Microsoft in 2018, organisations applying AI to their processes outperform laggards by 5% on factors like productivity, performance and business outcomes.

Among DataIQ Leaders, the range of automation projects being developed indicates the scope of the opportunity, from data wrangling and reporting through to personalisation of communications and rostering shifts for delivery drivers. All identified that a key starting point for automation is to identify low-hanging fruit – a target process which is either currently expensive to operate or not performing as desired. By applying automation, a use case can be made that acts as a proof of concept for an extension of smart technology into the organisation.

One grocery retailer had the benefit of board-level support and was able to land some quick wins. In one example, a store trading report was being created 364 days a year and required one full-time employee to deliver it. That person was a qualified accountant but was not able to add any value to the report, which was manually emailed to a distribution list.

The report was automated and is now created with zero human intervention and is achieving 99.9% accuracy. Prior to the creation of its centralised data and analytics function, the retailer had tried and failed to automate this task for ten years. The reason for this failure was the way the challenge was being looked at – automation of a flawed process, rather than scoping out what was needed and automating it as a new process. This has saved 600 hours of human effort each year.

Reduction in total headcount is not necessarily the only outcome from automation. At one logistics company which has a unionised workforce and operates the largest road fleet in Europe, the intention is to share the benefits of automation by reducing the working week from 40 hours to 35 eventually. It also has a recruitment issue to confront – the average age of drivers is 55 and younger workers are not choosing commercial vehicle driving as a career. That makes progress towards automated vehicles essential for its business survival.

Best practice for data democratisation

Another way to reduce the routine workload for data teams is to hand-off data access and reporting to business users on a self-service basis. This democratisation process has been significantly enabled by data extraction and reporting tools that have automation at their heart, meaning data can be explored by non-technical users within an appropriate wrapper of data governance.

Self-service BI and analysis can form a central enabling pillar for data literacy programmes because they show, rather than tell, users the power of insights derived from the data asset. Understanding of what can be discovered gradually increases within the organisation, laying the basis for a new data culture around evidence-based decision-making.

Real estate services firm Jones Lang LaSalle (JLL) has been on a five-year journey of data democratisation using BI tools and self-service as a driver of cultural change. It has reported that creating a data literate workforce generated $50 million worth of documented benefits to the business over a five-year period, for example.

To ensure that data teams are able to pass access to users efficiently and avoid creating a new workload of service support, there are golden rules to follow which improve the chances of success.

Rule 1 – Demand does not equal data competence

Individual data leaders, decision-makers and practitioners have grown used to being hands-on with business information. Most organisations similarly have significant groups of super-users of tools in which data and information can be stored and analysed, most evidently in the case of Excel. Within the specific realm for which this is being used, those practitioners may be highly proficient. But the data they are using may not conform to agreed standards, definitions, permissions and lineage, for example. These islands of data usage need to be identified and absorbed into the centrally managed data asset under the supervision of the data department to ensure what users access meets the corporate specification.

Rule 2 – Avoid code

Early data literacy programmes took the view that business leaders and senior executives should learn to code. In doing so, it was thought they would gain a better understanding of data and what it can do for the organisation. This is an error – the time spent learning a coding language is better applied to developing critical thinking skills, especially given the risk that any language learned may become redundant. Self-service tools now require little or no code – all of the back-end effort involved is managed by the data department and IT to ensure performance.

Rule 3 – Keep critical expertise centralised

Part of the goal of data literacy programmes is to drive up overall numeracy in order to help avoid simple errors in the interpretation of data and statistics. One multi-line insurance provider noted that it is struggling with data democratisation because of the risk that users can misinterpret BI if they are not data literate and numerate.

This is where a central analytics office or function has an important role to play by setting standards and vetting models before they become widely disseminated. In fact, building out a library of models can be a core enabler of self-service analytics by removing both the toil and the risk involved.

Similarly, data governance has to be kept in a central function and operated as the gatekeeper for any data source being admitted into the self-service environment. This does not necessarily mean it should be within the data department – it may fit better into compliance or even IT.

Rule 4 – The tool is not the outcome

Data democratisation should not be viewed as an end in itself. The purpose is to allow business users to answer routine, repeatable questions for themselves, releasing time for data teams to focus on innovation. This should be a mutual process since the more self-service access lines of business gain, the more data literate they become and therefore the more likely they are to ask more complex questions or to look for more innovative projects.

Political democracy is based around progress towards improved standards for the population and the economy and this is as true within business as it is within society. Technology is inherently neutral – it is the purpose to which it is put which gives it value.

Looking over the horizon

Automating today the tasks that were established yesterday is essential for data teams who want to innovate. At the same time, they also need to be looking ahead to tomorrow and scanning the horizon for the next data-led opportunities. While the data department does not operate in the same way as R&D, it can still incubate pioneering solutions, especially if it houses a data science function and allows a proportion of time to be given over to free exploration.

One major initiative that can support this is a partnership with academia, especially by building links with universities that run analytics, data science or related courses. These have expanded significantly in number in recent years and a key feature of most is an appetite for access to real-world problems and data. Many organisations now have two-way arrangements under which data practitioners set problems and teach on courses, while students are given the opportunity to work in a live industrial environment.

Santander has gone further than most by pledging in 2019 to hand over £30 million in funding for a new university in Milton Keynes, which will have 5,000 students and be the UK's first university focused on digital and data science skills. Similarly, the University of Cambridge has established the Cambridge Centre for Data-Driven Discovery (C2D3), a hub intended to harness the knowledge of academics in data science, ethics and a wide range of disciplines. C2D3 will allow experts across a number of areas, including those with technical, mathematical and topic knowledge, to work together on tackling the methodological and practical challenges presented by handling large data sets. It will be funded by a series of collaborations with up to ten partners in business and industry, with insurance giant Aviva the founding partner. The company will sponsor a research fellowship and support PhD students to help investigate some of the ethical, political and operational questions surrounding the use of data. The relationship is intended to help Aviva to develop new ethical approaches to advising customers through evidence-based science, while enabling university researchers to develop methods and tools to address real-world problems.

Although usually the preserve of data leaders, initiatives such as the Silicon Valley Singularity University also offer a strong blend of knowledge transfer and social networking. It has established itself as a global learning and innovation community using exponential technologies to tackle the world's biggest challenges and build a better future for all.

As a bare minimum, it is important that data teams engage with conferences and events as a way of keeping up to speed with the accelerating pace of innovation. Not least because these are often where senior executives first encounter the 'shiny new toys' which they then hand over to the data department to create.

DATA LITERACY STEPCOUNTER

Data teams need to look outside of their current boundaries and demands in order to grow and keep their own skills fresh.

Shouldering-off repetitive tasks to automation and self-service opens up space for innovation and helps to build data literacy among business stakeholders.

Steps 23–26:

23. Consider organising data teams into squads and tribes (if the department is of a sufficient size).

24. Encourage all data teams to engage widely with the business and beyond as this improves the flow of information in and out.

25. Keep telling the organisation what data has done and what more it could do.

26. Identify opportunities to automate processes within the data department in order to free data teams for more value-adding activities.

CHAPTER 8
Data individuals

Roadmap – in this chapter:

- Individuals possess positive and negative traits that can make or break the data team.

- Skills need to be kept fresh and each project used as a learning opportunity. A broad spectrum of skills is essential, not just specific technical abilities.

- A personal brand gives credibility, visibility and accessibility to data practitioners.

- Data individuals – especially data scientists – can be at the heart of digital transformations, but cultural obstacles can prevent this from happening.

- To continue to develop as individuals (and as a department), data practitioners need to challenge themselves and seek out new opportunities across the business. This may extend to further education, such as doing a Masters.

Engage

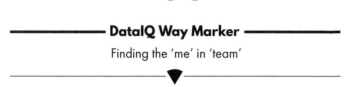

DataIQ Way Marker

Finding the 'me' in 'team'

How to be a team player

THE NEXT TIME you hear a motivational speaker say, 'there is no "I" in team', tell them they are wrong – 'me' and 'am' can both be found with a low degree of anagrammatical skill. This is not just a semantic argument. It goes to the heart of how many management disciplines view the role of the individual within a group. The common view is that the individual needs to be subsumed within the whole to avoid the risk of a singular talent over-shadowing the rest. As is routinely said in the world of sport, 'no player is bigger than the club'.

While this is a valid viewpoint when considering how to balance the needs of players against the needs of the club – such as setting an overall salary cap when assembling a squad – it fails to recognise the transformative impact that one individual can have. To a team finding it hard to score goals, finding a great striker matters. So does having the right partner to provide assists. If the team is shipping too many goals, then look to strengthen the midfield or defence. If these individual talents adopt and deliver the shape and gameplay set out by the manager, then you have a winning team.

So how does an individual data practitioner take their place within a data team and ensure their abilities mesh with those of their colleagues? In all likelihood, the current role they perform is because of a set of technical abilities they already possess and successes they have delivered by deploying them. But then, so has everybody else in the data team.

What turns a group of people with great skills into a high-performing team is cohesion. Interactions between individuals, a supportive culture, the willingness to lend a hand (or step back when appropriate) – these are signs that the team has bonded and found its way of working.

To make this happen, the individual (and their data leader) needs to understand the positive and negative aspects of their personality. A useful tool in this regard is DISC – it has a long history and extensive data to support its clustering of personality types into four major groups, each with a positive and negative aspect. Table 8.1 shows the styles and the traits that contribute to them.

Table 8.1A: DISC styles – positive aspects

Dominance – D-style	Influence – I-style
Enjoys winning and personal success	Optimistic outlook
Action-oriented and enjoys challenges	Collaborative
Works at pace	Upbeat and energetic
Self-confident	Expressive
Independent	Spontaneous
	Enjoys group activities and social interaction

Conscientiousness – C-style	Steadiness – S-style
Values precision and detail	Values support
Expert	Patient
Starter-finisher	Friendly
Systematic	Open to compromise
Values quality and standards	Consistent worker
Rational	Sincere
Keen to develop skills	Good listener

Table 8.1B: DISC styles – negative aspects

Dominance – D-style	Influence – I-style
Impatient	Inattentive
Opinionated	Animated
'In your face'	Lacks focus
Demanding/aggressive	Repeats questions
Low threshold	'Butterfly mind'
Snap decisions	Disorganised

Conscientiousness – C-style	Steadiness – S-style
Reserved	Resists new ideas or change
Quiet	Keeps opinions to themselves
Overly cautious	Needs space
Fears criticism	'Let me think about it'
Sceptical	Gives in too easily
Can become isolated	Avoids confrontation
Emotional under pressure	Slow to respond

To meld the personal abilities of each individual into that of a cohesive team requires amplification of positive aspects and reduction of the negative ones. Achieving this may require support in the form of mentoring or additional soft skills training, but the impact on a team and its performance is nearly always one of considerable uplift.

——————— **DataIQ Way Marker** ———————

What got you here won't keep you here

▼

Staying in the data swim

The skillset that got an individual into their current role in a data team may be a powerful foundation for their current practice. But things change. Data is a rapidly-evolving domain with new business challenges, fresh data sources, advances in data technology and new mathematical or statistical techniques constantly emerging.

As a data practitioner, it is important to keep those skills sharp in order to maintain the value they create for the team, stakeholders and organisation. The biggest risk is getting stuck in a constantly repeating cycle of BAU tasks that do not offer opportunities to stretch out into new challenges or develop new abilities on the back of each project.

As part of being an engaged team player, the individual data practitioner should look both within the organisation and externally for ways to refresh and enhance that skillset. If this is not already part of a structured career development plan created for the data practitioner by their data leader, then they need to challenge for it.

Leveraging internal resources

Data literacy can be developed both within the data department and across the organisation by ensuring these interactions take place:

- *Cross-team knowledge sharing* – each data team member likely possesses both matching and different skills. Learning from each other is hugely valuable and efficient, not least because it tends to happen in a live environment where those new learnings can be built in a known context.

- *Cross-function knowledge sharing* – what works for one tribe could have real benefits for another, but only if it is visible. Ensure success stories and show-and-tells are part of how communities of practice engage with each other.

- *Cross-departmental knowledge sharing* – understanding how other disciplines think about and use data can highlight untapped areas of existing skillsets or identify where new abilities need to be learned. If the individual data practitioner isn't across financial data or behavioural data, for example, it makes sense to take a look or seek out a project where they can learn about them.

- *Cross-organisation knowledge sharing* – data academies are a growth area and often focus on up-skilling non-data practitioners. Data practitioners may be asked to present or teach within this environment, but don't assume the rest of the curriculum is not relevant to them. Take a look at what's on offer.

Leveraging external resources

Data literacy needs to keep pace with developments across the data industry in order to remain current. Support this with the following activities:

- *Vendor training* – all tech vendors run their own certification programmes, which are valuable for building a deep understanding of how to apply these tools to tasks. Just be sure that individuals do not become 'badge collectors' without considering whether vendor-agnostic technical training has something to offer, or focusing only on the organisation's existing tech stack. The tools that are needed tomorrow could be very different.

- *Academic outreach* – research within the academic community tends to go deep into a very specific domain. This is an opportunity to discover more about a technique or process by engaging with institutions as an industry partner, providing a live environment for experiments as part of a knowledge exchange.

- *Soft skills training* – all the technical abilities in the world have no value if the data practitioner cannot communicate why they are relevant to stakeholders and the wider organisation. Make sure individuals are building a portfolio of soft skills that makes the data team easy and valuable to work with for stakeholders.

- *Window on world* – it is easy to see skills development as solely about the immediately applicable and practical. But all data work has real-world dimensions which may be easier to understand and address if practitioners kept abreast of what's happening in economics, society, culture. The legendary advertising guru David Ogilvy, founder of the ad agency that bears his name, said: "The most difficult people to find are those who have the capacity to become good copywriters. I have found that they always have well-furnished minds." Swap the word 'copywriters' for 'data practitioners' and it remains true.

Creating a personal data brand

"I started off in retail at Tesco, where I was always known as the 'data guy', providing insights into performance through coloured Post-it notes on brown paper." So says Paul Chapman, now head of CS global performance management at property services company JLL. That ability to communicate using simple tools gained him visibility and buy-in, a skill which he continues to apply even in the hugely complicated realm of global performance dashboards.

That is a good basis on which any data practitioner should build their brand. Data can seem like a closed world to non-data people and its processes often look black box in nature. That can dissuade business leaders and managers from seeking out the support and help they really need.

A personal brand is simply the way in which a data practitioner presents themself to the world and how the world then perceives that individual. As part of overall skills development, data practitioners should become conscious of this perception filter. A good way into this is to ask how the data team, data leader or business stakeholder would complete this sentence: 'I can be relied on to...'

The next step is to think about what the individual would want the answer to be. It could be transactional, such as always completing a task on time or finding the best way to visualise data. It could be emotional, such as building trust with stakeholders or keeping their word. Or it might be social, such as bringing cakes to the Friday wrap-up meeting.

Just as with any branded product or service, the personal brand is shorthand for many different aspects of the expectations and demands which stakeholders and colleagues bring into every interaction. By thinking about what their personal brand can be, individuals are saving everybody around them cognitive effort in deciding whether they are their 'data guy' or 'data gal'.

Enable

———— DataIQ Way Marker ————
Become an agent of change

▼

Supporting digital transformation

Until 2020, digital transformation was a planned strategy for organisations with a clear roadmap, timeline and milestones. Between 2018 and 2020, the proportion of organisations who were aiming to transform the whole enterprise to be digital-first rose from 31% to 41%, according to DataIQ research, indicating the accelerating pace of these projects. Even where planned, however, most organisations have little choice given the digital-first proposition of their disruptor rivals and fundamental changes to customer behaviour.

The Covid-19 pandemic removed any sense of choice as the impact of working from home and non-essential retail closures led to massive increases in demand for digital services and usage of e-commerce. If the previous 33% upswing in the pace of digital transformations over three years looked rapid, what happened in the 12 months of 2020 was hectic.

For data practitioners, this not only drove up demand for core services, such as dashboards, reporting and data platforms, but it also opened up entirely new opportunities to demonstrate the art of the possible. Louis DiCesari, global head of data, analytics and AI at Levi Strauss & Co, provides two examples from the response of that brand retailer: "While our stores were closed, we turned our European website into a lab, testing all of the promotion strategies we always wanted to try, but couldn't because of cross-channel complexities. We learned what worked where and we generated better price elasticity data than we ever had before.

"We didn't just let our stores sit closed, we turned them into micro fulfilment centres, leveraging AI-enabled ship-from-store capabilities to fulfil online orders and move through inventory. Of online demand in May 2020, 30% was fulfilled by stores, contributing to e-commerce growth of 79% that month."

Using an unprecedented disruption to the market to explore data-driven opportunities such as multi-variate testing and AI is a prime example of how data practitioners should think. The data leader needs to see data as an enabler for the business both in its as-is state and also in its to-be state. Long-desired target operating models may suddenly become a reality as a result of external factors.

Whether planned or forced, it is clear that organisations very much view data as a core component of their digital transformations. As Figure 8.1 shows, 80.4% expect a key benefit from their programme to be integrated customer data (38.1% expect a significant benefit, 42.3% a lot of benefit), while 89.5% say their decisions will be supported by data (48.4% significantly and 41.1% a lot). This view of data as a strategic pillar of digital transformation is an important opportunity for the data department and reflects growing maturity across organisations in their adoption of this resource.

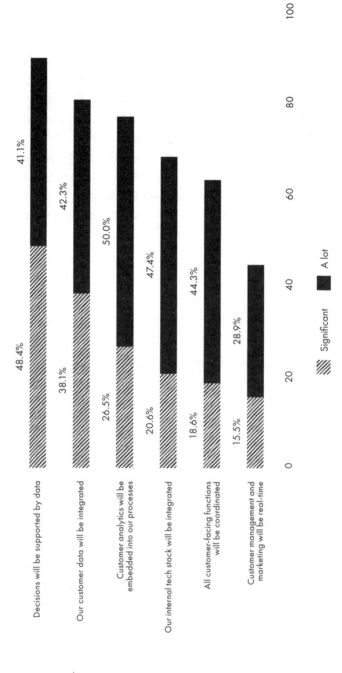

Figure 8.1: What level of benefit do you expect to gain from these aspects of digital transformation?

But it should not be assumed that a data practitioner is automatically viewed as having a central role in this way. Much depends on where the organisation is on its journey towards being data native at the point where it starts a digital transformation (or has one thrust upon it).

DataIQ researched the issue of how to get data science – often a key innovator that drives digital transformation – transferred into production. What the survey revealed is that culture factors make up three out of five of the biggest challenges identified. Significantly, a lack of understanding of data science within the business emerged as the leading challenge, even above legacy infrastructure (39.5% vs 38.4% – see Figure 8.2). This underlines just how important it is for data teams to demonstrate the art of the possible to stakeholders, as discussed in Chapter 7.

Similarly, the issue of conflict between data science and IT, as identified by 33.6%, shows how difficult it is to establish data as an accepted and engaged department. Assuming, that is, that enough data practitioners can be recruited, trained and retained – some 32.7% struggle to staff up their data science function. Again, this is where a positive data culture helps because it makes the organisation more appealing to candidates and incumbent practitioners.

Figure 8.2: What are your biggest data science challenges?

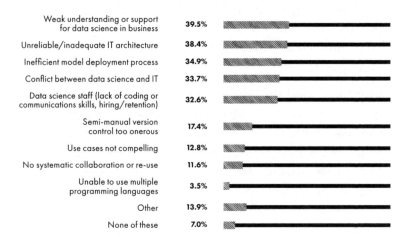

Weak understanding or support for data science in business	39.5%
Unreliable/inadequate IT architecture	38.4%
Inefficient model deployment process	34.9%
Conflict between data science and IT	33.7%
Data science staff (lack of coding or communications skills, hiring/retention)	32.6%
Semi-manual version control too onerous	17.4%
Use cases not compelling	12.8%
No systematic collaboration or re-use	11.6%
Unable to use multiple programming languages	3.5%
Other	13.9%
None of these	7.0%

Becoming a data champion

One way to avoid these obstacles to getting data accepted as an enabler of digital transformation is by becoming a data champion – the voice of data in every conversation within the business (and potentially across the sector or industry as a whole). This does not just mean being active as part of BAU engagement with stakeholders. A data champion makes data accessible, appealing and personal. That might seem to be a role solely for a data leader, but at every level, data practitioners can have an impact by behaving in this way.

Leanne Allen is a good example of what this means. Her day job is within Barclaycard International's DASA (data and strategic analytics) department as head of data partners for cards and payments. This is a very demanding role in which she is accountable for all the external merchant reporting that is processed daily on the company's platform. Allen is also a data subject matter expert for Barclays Payments Acquiring and is often the go-to person for high-profile projects.

But Barclaycard realised there was a need to kick-start new data conversations to keep the business going forward. With the aim of connecting colleagues outside of the data department to the world of data and letting them explore how data can be a useful asset, the DASA team wanted to encourage colleagues to partner with them to improve ways of working. The solution was a Data Festival involving three live events across the company's UK sites in Fleet, Canary Wharf and Northampton during early 2020.

Allen arranged for colleagues from DASA and external vendors to showcase the power of data and reporting tools available to colleagues. While many data-oriented events brand themselves as festivals, in this case the theme was fully realised. The team from DASA jumped on the theme and created eight interactive and fun stalls to bring their data work to life for colleagues, from the 'pricing mosh pit', to 'selfies with the DASA rock stars' to 'tour promoters pushing strategy and decisions'. Even the entry gate featured a disco ball and attendees received a festival wristband. It was standing room only at each event with more than 540 colleagues in person or connecting with content globally. Colleagues from the USA and Germany were also able to view the events via a webcast.

Stretch

———————— DataIQ Way Marker ————————

Let your reach exceed your grasp (but not by too much...)

"Our finest self won't materialise without challenge, without our being pushed to our limits. And, much more important than the challenge itself, are the traits and skills we develop when rising to it."

– Maja Petrovic, Psychology of Challenges

From the comfort zone to the challenge zone

Given the experience we have all been through with the Covid-19 pandemic, it is entirely understandable to want to remain in our comfort zone, surrounded by the familiar and following well-established routines. After all, with so many unknowns and genuine perils in the outside world, it is a natural reaction to seek stability and control in our internal world.

For data practitioners, data teams and the data department as a whole, however, settling into the tried-and-tested is risky. BAU will not sustain either the funding or intellectual needs of this domain. Automation will continually take over from human activity across the board, leading to a reduced need for headcount. Boredom will erode productivity and retention, leading to more open positions or positions staying unfilled for longer.

The only way to avoid this death spiral is to stretch. As an individual, this means moving towards the challenge zone, seeking out activities and projects that are demanding, may require new skills, but are also likely to deliver a significant reward emotionally and in business terms. In data terms, these are relatively easy to identify since automation, AI, ML and the rest all require significant stretch by both data practitioners and the organisation. Recalling the challenges identified around data science in Figure 8.2, there is still a lot of work to be done in bringing these tools into the production environment.

What is often harder for individuals is to recognise when self-limiting thoughts are keeping them in their comfort zone, rather than having a self-realising mindset. Maintaining emotional equilibrium and pursuing vulnerability management are normal, natural responses to change and threats. But these can be reinforced – and therefore need to be challenged and overcome – by a range of other factors, including:

- *Past failure* – all data practitioners will have worked on projects that failed to land. Depending on the circumstances, this can feel traumatic, leading to the avoidance in future of anything that looks risky. One way this can be tackled is by the data leader building a 'no blame' culture and for the data team to acknowledge that 'we win together, we lose together'. Both of these absolve individuals from personal worry (assuming there was no avoidable or deliberate error, of course).

- *Pursuit of perfection* – many data practitioners want their work to reach the ideal outcome. When scoping new tasks, complexity or difficult circumstances can make it seem that this will be impossible to achieve, leading to avoidance. But if the global healthcare crisis has a lesson to teach data practitioners, it is that 'good enough now' beats 'wait until it's perfect'. Be ready to accept the 80% outcome, rather than hoping for the 100%.

- *'Can't do' mindset* – without knowing it, all of us can fall into thinking, 'I can't do that' when something looks difficult or complex. The truth is that we are capable of more than we know. All it requires is the right enablers, a supportive environment, colleagues to work with and an acceptance that, 'maybe I can do that'. If you don't try, you'll never know…

- *Fear of rejection* – the opinion of others may be a factor in the individual's inner voice telling them not to try something new just in case they get judged negatively. This is where the data team has a major role to play in creating a supportive culture that reassures individuals they are accepted. If the data leader can persuade the organisation to lose its own fear of failure and adopt test-and-learn as a working practice, so much the better.

Setting career goals

Stretch targets and moving into the challenge zone are not just for data projects – they can be personal objectives. Much depends on how the individual views their career and the goals they have set for themself. As we considered in Chapter 6, learning about Career Anchors can provide a valuable insight into the types of role to which an individual is suited.

Nearly every data role involves a degree of stretch just because of the nature of this practice. Some offer more of the comfort zone that comes with a strong, established skillset, while others are much more demanding. The critical thing is to silence the inner voice which worries about how the individual will be judged. For example, there is nothing wrong with wanting to stay hands-on with data work, such as staying within the analytics environment. Organisations are increasingly realising they need to create career paths which do not automatically take individuals away from what they are good at in order to gain seniority and pay rises. While there will naturally be ceilings, this may well suit an individual if they enter a lifestage where family life becomes much more important, either because they are a parent or a carer, for example.

Even if the data practitioner stays in the comfort zone of their abilities, it is still possible to stretch themself as a person and as a practitioner. For example, they might take on the role of mentor to younger practitioners or as a tutor to colleagues elsewhere in the business who are up-skilling themselves in data. Alternatively, they might get involved in external stretching activities, such as volunteering their data skills to the third sector, taking a secondment in the public sector, or joining one of the many steering committees and working groups looking into data and AI ethics.

Any one of these will require stepping into a challenge zone, such as leading a meeting or speaking in public. The thing to remember is that everything the individual now does within their comfort zone once felt challenging, but has since become comfortable. You don't know whether you really can't do something until you try!

Personal stretch goals do not necessarily have to be major, however. Professor Andy Neely, Pro-Vice-Chancellor – enterprise and business relations, University of Cambridge, says: "A piece of career advice I'd give anyone is, don't just strive for one big thing. Take pleasure from lots of small achievements on the way. It's the small achievements that give you the motivation to keep going."

Within the perspective of stretching the organisation, a degree of caution is also advisable. While awareness of leading-edge ideas and techniques are important to the health of the data department, the resources of the organisation are finite and timescales for experiments tend to be much shorter than those in academia. Passion projects should be fitted into personal time (or work time that has been allowed for R&D) until it becomes clear whether there is a commercial benefit that can be taken to potential stakeholders.

Should I do a Masters?

A notable feature of recent years has been the emergence of formal, academic qualifications in data (including data science). It is now possible to build on degree-level technical skills, re-skill or up-skill from non-technical disciplines, or validate abilities that have been developed in role by studying for a Masters (MSc).

Recognising this, many organisations have built support and funding for these qualifications into the career plans they offer to practitioners at a certain level of their employment, usually after a minimum number of years in post. This can be valuable to underpin the authority of the data office and its members. Similarly, it can be a useful way to sense-check and refresh knowledge after a long period of focus on familiar activities. Obviously, a Masters can be used as a stretch exercise which requires taking on a new challenge.

Some care does need to be taken about which Masters course to follow. Even a cursory glance at the curricula offered will reveal a wide variety of content and very different areas of emphasis. In some cases, these courses have been consciously designed for those looking to transfer into data as a career. Others have a strong technology orientation, while yet more are based in statistical techniques. Due diligence is advised before embarking on one.

Deciding whether to take advantage of the option to do a Masters which might be on offer – or whether to fund one personally – is again a reflection of the individual's personal career goals. Having a Masters is not solely about status and career advancement – it can be a way to re-skill having recognised that the data domain is significantly different from the one the individual entered at the start of their career. Self-learning may be more appropriate, or the practitioner may need the discipline of a structured course and tutor.

DATA LITERACY STEPCOUNTER

Career-long learning is as important for data practitioners as for any other professional, especially to remain data literate.

The organisation itself needs to be kept data literate as a continual activity.

Steps 27–29:

27. Encourage individual data practitioners to identify their personality type and work on having a balanced data team.

28. Put in place training to keep skillsets up to date and ahead of the demand curve.

29. Keep stretching the capabilities and reach of data practitioners to avoid falling into the trough of business as usual.

CHAPTER 9
Data and economic value

Roadmap – in this chapter:

- The value of the data economy in the EU plus UK was €400bn in 2020.

- Methodologies for valuing data lag behind the practice of applying data to value creation.

- Governments are increasingly looking at how to tax digital activity, including the value created by data.

- Data leaders need to decide on a method for attributing value to their data activities, even if this is only at the level of recognising a percentage of incremental revenue.

Macro-economics

————————— **DataIQ Way Marker** —————————

Data has a value (but struggles to be valued)

▼

Core concepts of the value of data

ONE THING EVERYBODY in business agrees on – data is valuable.

According to the European Data Market Monitoring Tool, published by the European Commission's Directorate-General for Communications Networks, Content and Technology in 2020, the value of the data market (the market where digital data is exchanged as products or services derived from raw data) for the 27 members states in the EU plus the UK was €75bn, up 4.9% on the previous year. At the higher level of the data economy (including the economic impacts generated by the data market) the value was over €400 billion and growing at 7.6% per year. In the UK, the data economy accounted for 4% of total GDP. Clearly, data is an engine of economic growth.

Investors have recognised this fact – a study by PwC in 2019 ('Putting a Value on Data' by Neil Hampson, www.pwc.co.uk/data-analytics/documents/putting-value-on-data.pdf) found that data-driven organisations tended to have higher stock market valuations than peers in the same industry, while those with mature data and analytics capabilities are twice as likely to be in the top quartile for performance in their industry sector.

This positive lens is not just focused on the revenue-generating potential of data. The concept of data as an asset has grown in popularity since 2011 when the World Economic Forum published its report, *Personal Data: The Emergence of a New Asset Class*. By

2020, the European Commission put a total asset value for personal data alone across the EU27 plus UK of more than €1 trillion.

But there is a problem and a paradox – while everybody agrees on the value of data, nobody can agree how to value it.

The problem lies with the accountancy profession where data is classified as an intangible asset. Historically, a broad view was taken of this category in order to account for the difference between a company's valuation (specifically during a takeover) and its physical or monetary assets – the often sizeable gap between the two was once assigned to goodwill. From the 1980s onward, brand valuation emerged as a core intangible asset that in many cases held most of the value of a business. Accountancy standards allowed the brand to be put on the balance sheet during the course of a merger or acquisition along with other physical assets, but with one crucial difference – brands do not have their value amortised over time or across their useful economic life.

These same accounting standards also allow for data to be valued as an intangible asset in the same merger and acquisition circumstances, but in a highly reductive way as 'customer lists'. Not only is this definition very limiting – a large proportion of the value realised by the use of data comes from non-personal data sources – but valuations are reached using one of three approaches: cost, income, market. Both cost and market valuations produce very low outcomes since organisations anticipate a significantly high ratio of return on investment from their spending on data (cost-based approach) and are highly unlikely ever to sell their 'customer list' separately from the business (market approach). Income-based valuations are very complex, in essence, subtracting the present value of cost-based returns from every operating function (e.g. manufacturing, distribution, IT, HR, R&D, etc.) and any other identifiable intangibles (e.g. brand value) from the value of the business. The residue is then assumed to represent non-contractual customer relationships. Again, this approach only considers this one asset type and ignores all other forms of data.

Economists have long recognised that value is generated from data in a number of important ways:

- *Non-rivalry* – data can be used multiple times without degrading its value, unlike a raw material, such as the oil to which it is often compared in a widely used expression.

- *Externalities* – combining disparate data types and sources to generate value with a higher multiple than each individual set would deliver.

- *Generality* – supporting multiple different decisions or processes from the same data.

Each of these acts to enhance where and how value can be created from the same data asset.

Yet despite the best efforts of organisations as focused on this issue as the World Economic Forum, Open Data Institute, Institute of Practitioners in Advertising, DMA UK and countless commercial consultancies, none has so far been able to create an accepted, standard valuation framework.

This forces each organisation to undertake its own approach without the expectation that it will be signed off by the finance and accounting teams. As an example of what such a valuation might look like – and what is involved in reaching it – Forbes referenced Highways England and its CDO Davin Crowley-Sweet in an article published in 2021 ('Data Valuation Paves the Road to the Future for Highways England' by Douglas B. Laney, www.forbes.com/sites/douglaslaney/2021/02/01/data-valuation-paves-the-road-to-the-future-for-highways-england/?sh=774b46b8612c). In 2018, the agency had a balance sheet valued at £300bn of which £115bn was accounted for by intangible assets. Through a rigorous process of mapping key data assets to business functions and their financial value (cost and income), alongside an assessment of each data asset's potential market value, Crowley-Sweet emerged with an asset valuation for data of £60bn. Even so, data still does not feature on the formal balance sheet at Highways England.

Taxing data's value

All of the estimates of data's value have attracted significant interest from governments around the world. Finding a new driver of economic growth, especially one with the quasi-magical property of yielding value while not being consumed, is highly attractive to policymakers. The UK has published a National Data Strategy alongside its National Digital Strategy out of recognition of the opportunities it presents and the mutual relationship between both, for example.

Where economic value is being created, the interest of tax authorities is certain to follow. This is where the absence of a modern accounting standard for data as an asset is likely to become problematic. As noted earlier, when brand value became formally recognised as intellectual property and could be added to balance sheets when a company was being bought, sold or merged, many brand owners realised a mistake had been made in not amortising this value across a given period. As a result, tax mitigation cannot be applied by showing impairment to the brand value annually, for example, or value engineering applied to increase the price of a business during takeover negotiations. In consequence of this, many brands do not undergo formal valuation and recognition as an intellectual property asset.

Digital taxation (or tax on digital transactions) seems highly likely to be a feature of the 2020s to help fund the support given by government to business during the Covid-19 crisis (and also to claw back some of the profits made by digital platforms). When this happens, taxation of data seems likely to follow out of a recognition that data is a key resource of the digital economy.

As with the valuation of data, this immediately throws up conceptual issues about where tax might be applied. While profit is an obvious target, productivity and output from labour is another option. The

French Ministry of the Economy and Finance considered this in 2013 in a report by its task force on the taxation of the digital economy: "The digital economy has stepped outside the theory of the firm: it is possible to 'work' the users of an application, in the same way as suppliers and employees were 'worked' in the past. The fact that users receive no monetary consideration for their activity explains some of the dramatic productivity gains of the digital economy."

While individual countries figure out how to tax the profits of digital platforms – not an easy task given the complex structures and internal cross-charging they adopt – one proposal made by the task force was that, "collecting data obtained through regular and systematic monitoring of users is the only taxable event that ensures the neutrality of the tax with regard to business models, technologies and business location strategies … The proposal does not consist of taxing data collection per se. Instead, the aim is to create a tax incentive for businesses to adopt practices with regard to collecting and using data obtained from users."

This idea was not adopted in France and, for now, the idea of directly taxing data or the 'free labour' carried out by users of digital services and the excess value they provide by giving their data has not returned to the spotlight.

But one thing is certain – where value is being created, taxation will surely follow. And perhaps with it, an appropriate accounting standard that puts a proper level of valuation on this asset.

Measuring the benefit

──────────── **DataIQ Way Marker** ────────────

Pick a number, then prove it

▼

Developing data metrics

Most data leaders will not need to concern themselves with the intricacies of accounting for intangible assets or taxation rates for data collection. A more pressing concern is how to demonstrate to the organisation – and specifically to the chief financial officer – that there is a positive return on investment from data. Operating as a cost centre may be allowable in the short term – data and analytics enjoyed a relatively prolonged honeymoon phase during the 2010s and some functions, such as data science, still do.

In DataIQ research in H2 of 2020, 4.9% of organisations said they were still running data science as a cost centre, for example. By contrast, in a LinkedIn post in January 2021, Harry Powell, director of data and analytics at Jaguar Land Rover, put a figure of £100m annually against the revenue delivered to the business by his team.

Just as significantly, the same DataIQ study found 29.1% of organisations did not know what level of revenue uplift to expect from data science. At some point, all investments come under scrutiny and need to prove their worth, with the CFO likely to want to see a significant multiple of the costs involved as a return on investment, otherwise cash would be assigned to other projects.

While data is all about numbers, metrics can prove harder to establish. There is an inherent invisibility in the way data exists within a business – it is not viewed as an intangible asset for nothing. Business processes that fundamentally require data to operate can be lengthy to map end-to-end and involve multiple departments and even external partners, with data contributing to these processes at many different points along the value chain. Table 9.1 shows some examples across different sectors for customer-facing processes.

Table 9.1: Data activities by sector

Insurance	Customer data – risk models – pricing models – conversion forecasts – claims forecasts – settlement data – product profitability reporting – customer profitability reporting – customer lifetime value models
Retail/ e-commerce	Customer segmentation – customer personas – audience profiling – prospect matching – response tracking – conversion forecasting – conversion tracking – live stock tracking – returns reporting – product profitability reporting
Travel and leisure	Purchase history – purchase forecasting – pricing models – cross-sell models – destination data – proposition personalisation – service tracking – satisfaction tracking – destination and product profitability reporting

For all of these data components to support value creation, multiple business processes need to operate effectively. Separating the contribution made by data alone is likely to require sophisticated econometric modelling unless the individual steps can be specifically isolated and local metrics put in place. This may be possible around clear customer actions, such as cross-product purchasing in response to personalised marketing. But in most cases it is a complex process and few organisations have managed to develop robust, formal approaches.

In fact, anecdotal evidence from DataIQ revealed only one organisation at this level – the advanced analytics function of Royal Mail recruited an accountancy-qualified attribution manager to track financial outcomes back to data inputs. The leader of the function at the time also recognised that some data activities would continue to be cost centres, but looked to maintain a positive ROI at the top level across the portfolio of data projects being undertaken.

Interestingly, at Jaguar Land Rover, Powell defended data against strict financial measurement, noting that, "it can also limit the vision of the team if it is the only thing that is thought to matter. There are many useful applications of analytics which may be hard to link to profit, either because their effect is too diffuse or because the payback is in the following accounting period. You need to make sure that measurable profit is only part of your performance review."

At Highways England, Crowley-Sweet also recognised that data's impact could not be directly observed but has to be inferred from its impact on the processes it supports. This approach identified up to £1.2m in business efficiencies that could be achieved using data, with one specific insight leading to £20m in savings from a £300,000 investment in optimised maintenance interventions.

A number of approaches are used by data practitioners to try to identify the benefit they are delivering, many of them focused on the effects for which they are directly responsible. This does require carefully constructed metrics, benchmarking before and after the action taken and, ideally, control groups which are not exposed to the data-driven activity. While these hold-out cells are a long-established principle within direct marketing, few organisations are willing to go as far as stochastic experiments (or counterfactuals, as Powell calls them) which involved doing nothing at all in some situations and comparing this inactivity against those where an input has been applied.

The most commonly encountered solution used by data leaders is to win agreement from a business stakeholder at the outset of a project that a proportion of any incremental revenue generated (or costs saved if that is the nature of the project) will be recognised as coming from data. Picking a number – or rather agreeing on n% – to which both parties hold is considerably easier than formal attribution. It is also compelling within the organisation to have a stakeholder telling the story of how data created value, rather than the data leader making this claim.

There is a third path between operating as a value-creating department with formal attribution and accepting that data is a cost centre, which may be more acceptable – operating on a cost-neutral basis. In this approach, costs are acknowledged at the top level and offset by an agreed level of contribution from stakeholder-supported activities, but without having a specific target for value to be delivered. Some organisational cultures and CFOs are willing to allow this, but it does not build maturity in the adoption of data and analytics, neither does it create a platform from which the department can truly grow.

For Crowley-Sweet, leaving data's impact unmeasured was not an option or acceptable, hence the hard effort he made to identify effects and their financial value. As he told this author, these measurements "have turned data lambs into lions".

DATA LITERACY STEPCOUNTER

Becoming data literate also involves becoming financially literate – money is the language of business.

Data leaders need to focus on building a culture in which value creation from data is an agreed element of every project.

Steps 30–32:

30. Consider carefully whether data should be valued as an asset or whether to focus on value creation.

31. Work with stakeholders to win attribution to data usage of a percentage of incremental revenue achieved.

32. Include non-financial metrics in projects to reflect indirect impacts or longer-term outcomes.

CHAPTER 10
Values and ethics

Roadmap – in this chapter:

- Cambridge Analytica showed what could be done with big data when regulatory and ethical considerations were set aside.

- The impact has been to make many consumers more cautious about sharing their data – although some have simply become reckless.

- Transparency around data usage is vital as this helps to build trust but can be difficult when using a complex digital ecosystem.

- Monetisation and mobility are additional features of data usage that need to be considered and explained.

- Develop a data ethics framework that addresses the four foundational principles – autonomy, beneficence, non-maleficence and fairness – and also what sanctions might apply.

Data-value exchange

"And why beholdest thou the mote that is in thy brother's
eye, but considerest not the beam that is in thine own eye?"
– Matthew 7.3

The data-savvy consumer

FOR MOST OF the 2010s, data-driven businesses operated with a high degree of asymmetric power compared to their customers. That is, they were able to harvest huge volumes of information on everything from purchasing and preferences down to location, device and even the level of battery charge, with few obstacles and very little awareness among consumers that this was happening.

A presentation given at the DataIQ Future event in 2013 by Michal Kosinski, then deputy director of the University of Cambridge Psychometric Centre, revealed just what had become possible when 'big data' met data science. He started with the research question of whether psychological traits – in particular the 'big five' personality traits (openness, conscientiousness, extraversion, agreeableness, neuroticism) together with IQ – could be observed and measured in practice. Based on a research exercise using surveys delivered to Facebook users, called 'You are what you like', which generated over 250,000 profiles, he applied predictive analytical modelling techniques which showed that these traits could be identified based on the material which users liked on the social platform to a degree of confidence between 0.55 and 0.78.

But the study was able to take this even further by predicting those traits based on what individuals liked or disliked, with the levels of accuracy from the model's predictions reaching 0.95 for race, 0.93 for gender, between 0.77 and 0.88 for sexual orientation and, notably, 0.85 for likelihood to vote Democrat or Republican. His team developed a tool that was offered to marketing agencies and brands, called Magic Sauce, that could make robust inferences from a single Facebook like, enabling highly accurate targeting of ads on the social network and therefore more effective and efficient campaigns.

If there was an item in that last paragraph which set an alarm bell ringing in your mind, then you are right to heed it. Kosinski was not alone in working on this technique and one of his peers – Aleksandr Kogan – sold a similar solution to a then-nascent business called Cambridge Analytica which specialised in applying big data and data science to political campaigns. (Kosinski demurred from having his own work applied in the political realm on principle.) As is now only too familiar, this sophisticated profiling, targeting and campaigning approach, claiming to hold profiles on over 220 million US citizens alone, was deployed to apparently devastating effect, significantly influencing the outcomes of the US presidential election and the UK Brexit referendum in 2016.

What happened next is well known with a full-blown media storm in the wake of investigative journalism by Channel 4 and *The Guardian* which exposed the data tricks being used. While some political commentators questioned just how much impact micro-targeting of messages had on voting intentions, and many digital marketers argued that there was little harm in collecting data on preferences, this is to miss the most important point – that none of the consumers who responded to surveys on Facebook were aware that their answers could be used to profile their political, sexual, racial or other preferences (or indeed that their friends' data was being collected, too, via the access required by the survey app).

For regulators wanting to act, the timing of this scandal was in many ways ideal – the EU was in the process of adopting the GDPR during 2016 (with a two-year transition to enforcement in 2018) that shifted the balance of power between data controllers and data subjects. Consumer expectations of how their data is used, combined with accountability and transparency, became important considerations that all data-driven businesses needed to address through mechanisms like Privacy Impact Assessments, privacy notices and consent forms.

The effect on consumer attitudes can be clearly seen in tracking research carried out by DataIQ between 2016 and 2019 (see Figure 10.1). Nearly half of consumers had returned to a position of preferring not to share their personal data unless it was absolutely necessary (the Cautious group), whereas the number who were happy to share if provided with an explanation for why it was needed (the Rational) had halved. But perhaps most worrying of all was the emergence of those who either do not think about it or do not care – this 20.2% could be described as the Reckless. And they present a real challenge to data leaders when working out their data collection principles in tandem with legal and compliance teams because Reckless consumers are likely to click past privacy notices, leaving doubt as to whether their consent is genuinely informed or not.

Figure 10.1: Attitudes to data sharing – What best describes your attitude when a company asks for your personal information?

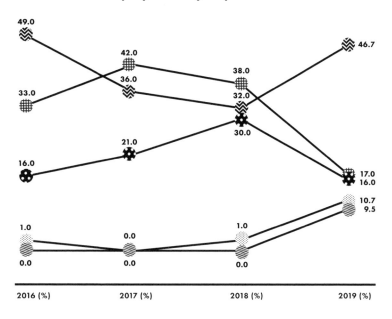

Taken together, the Cambridge Analytica scandal and the GDPR (or the CPPA in California and many similar pieces of legislation globally) mean that the 2020s started with consumers only too well aware that their data is being harvested and used, regardless of their attitude towards that activity. For data-driven businesses that means care is needed right along the data supply chain to ensure uses do not sit outside of reasonable expectations, however difficult it can sometimes be to define either of those things.

──────── **DataIQ Way Marker** ────────

Don't take personal data for granted

▼

Transparency

If individuals are to share their data with organisations, they expect to receive value in return. In many cases, this is received in kind through access to a free service (photo sharing, news feeds, etc.) or to facilitate the delivery of a paid service (age confirmation for adult content, for example). This data-value exchange is likely to be clear enough at the point where the consumer initiates the relationship. Indeed, the GDPR and similar data protection laws now mandate that organisations are transparent with their data subjects about the purpose, limitations and controls under which data is being captured.

Problems tend to arise later on as the relationship matures and the customer has built trust in the brand. Consumers stop checking up on what the organisation is doing with their data and take it on trust that it remains within the original bounds. As emerged in 2016 onwards, this trust was often misplaced and there was a profound lack of transparency in relation to data being captured across digital channels and devices.

For data leaders and their organisations, this is a major issue because opaque data practices erode trust, which in turn affects customer relationships, value creation and even performance. Among Australian CEOs surveyed by PwC in 2018 (in their report *Aligning Purpose to Restore Trust,* www.pwc.com.au/ceo-agenda/ ceo-survey/2018/aligning-purpose-to-restore-trust.html?utm_ campaign=sbpwc&utm_medium=site&utm_source=articletext), 65% said they were concerned about declining trust in business. Strikingly, only 18% thought this was a problem for their own organisation, with the rest viewing it as an issue for everybody else.

When defining the corporate data strategy to align with the business strategy, engaging with stakeholders around new data-driven processes, or reviewing data products and propositions through a data governance lens, holding this issue of trust in mind is critical. The more transparent the organisation is able to be with data subjects, the more likely they are to trust that their rights will be respected and to give consent. This may be achieved by clear indications of purpose, easy access to information and controls, or even just the use of plain language.

Where transparency becomes more difficult is when you need to step beyond first-party data and involve third-party sources, whether that is via audience matching on social media for marketing or enhancing customer data with overlays. In the digital marketing space especially, there are significant obstacles to transparency and therefore risks to trust – even the UK's data protection authority, the Information Commissioner's Office, found that the processes behind web serving and app provisioning were a Gordian knot which it could not find the Alexandrian axe to split.

This can lead to a difficult trade-off between maintaining the velocity of digital marketing and online services while having to trust in multiple third parties to operate in a transparent way. At a legal level, liability rests with the data controller and many of the intermediaries in the digital ecosystem are only too happy to pass on this responsibility to the brands using them. Even the major digital platforms tend to argue that they are simply 'dumb pipelines' for content, including ads, services and e-commerce, when it suits them. Deciding where to strike the right balance often reflects the risk appetite of the individual organisation and also the risk-reward ratio. As a data leader, this may not be your decision to make, but you do need to be aware of it and to offer wise counsel ahead of time.

Data monetisation and mobility

Before the introduction of the GDPR in 2018, data monetisation was a common part of data strategies, often used to help fund activities such as direct marketing, especially where resources were constrained (such as in the charity sector). Gaining consent for data to be shared with third parties in this way was one of the requirements of the new regulations and became much more challenging as a result, not least because consumers were relatively ill-informed about this practice. In DataIQ research carried out in 2019, 44.4% of a panel of 1,000 consumers said that they assumed a free service or app is paid for by ads, compared to only 16.3% who assumed the company would sell their personal data to pay for it.

A formerly thriving marketplace for personal data virtually collapsed in the wake of this legal change. But the opportunity to monetise personal data – and the potential demand for external information to enhance customer data – did not entirely go away. When DataIQ asked data leaders how the pandemic had impacted on their data strategies in 2020, 21.8% said they had identified gaps and filled them with third-party data, while 27.6% had also found gaps but not taken action. Especially at a time when customer behaviour and entire markets were changing rapidly, it was obvious that the view each organisation has from its own customer base alone does not provide the full picture, such as financial strain or headroom.

Helping to fill those gaps in customer knowledge has become a business opportunity for organisations that have large-scale data sets which cover a significant proportion of the population and also have a specific selling point. Examples of this are telcos, like Vodafone, which offer location-aware data and payment processors, such as Barclays Market and Customer Insights, which provide aggregated spend data at sector and geography level. Crucially, these data sets are put into the marketplace at an aggregated level which prevents individuals from being identified, using robust compliance and governance processes in order to satisfy data protection authorities and to reassure clients that usage is legitimate.

A new marketplace is also opening up around non-personal data types which are therefore not subject to regulation (provided they cannot be used to identify an individual such as through a specific device at a given time and location), but which also have potentially significant value to users. Internet of Things' data is one example where very high volumes are being generated from sensors and devices which may have value beyond the specific needs of those machines, such as to drive services in smart cities. Already, data exchanges exist within platforms like AWS where real-time data can be licensed and embed via APIs into external systems. Data leaders need to consider the possibility of exploiting such revenue streams when working out investment cases.

Alongside this, data ecosystems will become essential to support many innovative services where sole tenant data is not sufficient. This foregrounds a key issue around data mobility – how to ensure that individuals can bring their personal data into play in order to benefit from such services. Legislation and industry standards, such as the open banking in the UK, are helping to enable this. So, too, are initiatives like Ctrl-Shift's data mobility sandboxes where commercial organisations are able to explore the infrastructure and controls necessary when building out new propositions.

One example which the consultancy ran during 2020 brought together Public Health England, mental health charity Big White Wall and HSBC to explore how permissioned personal data mobility could improve the understanding of individual clinical situations and people's lives. With a working name of WellApp, the service was designed as a mass market proposition for preventative mental well-being which could be used in conjunction with more specialist clinical services integrated into the user's personal mental well-being journey. The service envisaged a tool for individuals to track and proactively self-manage their mental well-being, driven by personal behavioural data from a range of everyday digital services. As with data monetisation, data mobility and participation in these emerging ecosystems needs to be part of data strategy setting.

Data ethics

"We do not believe any group ... adequate enough or wise enough to operate without scrutiny or without criticism."
– Robert J. Oppenheimer

Ethical principles

Ethics can appear challenging as a subject for data leaders. For one thing, they offer an almost limitless scope for study, from entry-level primers right through to academic professorships. For another, they do not seem an obvious fit within the commercial environment or a clear fit with the standard issues that need to be addressed.

But ethics already have a place within business – every choice that is made which might have an impact on individuals, society, the environment or the economy has an inherent ethical dimension, whether this is recognised overtly or not. Choices go beyond legal compliance, not least because one choice may be to ignore legal restraints in order to pursue a profitable course of action. During the 2000s and 2010s, many organisations acted in ways that were both deliberately in contradiction of the law and were also unethical, from mis-selling of pensions and mortgages to trading in customer data without permission. Arbitrage of the financial penalties that regulators might impose against the potential revenue to be gained was a common practice.

Times change. So do markets and also customer expectations. Organisations that operate within an overtly ethical framework are now able to achieve benefits that do not exist for unethical firms, from charging a premium to achieving best-in-class performance.

Evidence for this can be found in a study carried out by global research agency Morningstar which compared 745 sustainable investment funds to 4,150 traditional funds and found they matched or beat returns in all categories, whether bonds or shares, UK or abroad.

According to the researchers, "Average returns and success rates for sustainable funds suggest that there is no performance trade-off associated with sustainable funds. In fact, a majority of sustainable funds have outperformed their traditional peers over multiple time horizons." Over the last ten years, the average annual return for a sustainable fund invested in large global companies has been 6.9% a year, while a traditionally invested fund has made 6.3% a year, according to Morningstar.

This underlines a key point about ethics – it is not a choice between doing good or being successful, but that the first of these is now a driver of the second.

──────── DataIQ Way Marker ────────

Not just data rights, but doing the right thing with data

For the data leader who wants to start to define the ethical stance of their department – and ideally be a part of the ethical discussion across the whole organisation – a good starting point is to consider four key principles that underpin ethics in all forms:

1. autonomy

2. beneficence

3. non-maleficence

4. fairness.

Each of these can be addressed within the context of data and needs to be considered when working out a code of data ethics.

1. Autonomy

Retaining control and being able to exercise personal decisions without coercion or negative consequences is a key dimension of ethics that is also written into data protection and privacy legislation. As individuals, citizens of the EU have a fundamental right to both of these, for example, which translates into rights such as the Right to be Forgotten, Right of Erasure or Right to Withdraw Consent. Obliging an individual to give up any of these rights during data capture and processing will potentially infringe those rights. So processes should be designed with ongoing autonomy in mind, such as ensuring access to a control centre, supporting engagement or transactions with minimal data exchange, or adopting decentralised data tools that leave ownership of the data with the individual while allowing for service and transactions to proceed.

2. Beneficence

Doing good for the data subject involves an ethical consideration of the desired commercial outcome to which data is being applied and the benefit that will be experienced. This applies as much to non-personal data as to personally identifiable information, so that recommendations made via a website or app are optimal to the individual, rather than solely in the interests of the business, for example. In many ways, this forces the level of data-driven decisioning to consider each individual, rather than dealing in groups and averages, which is not necessarily what the data architecture or operating processes are able to support. Yet keeping skills, tech and data at the most advanced level is itself an ethical choice which proves beneficence – consider how failure to update core information security software led to data breaches at Sony and BA, for example.

3. Non-maleficence

Probably the best-known example of any ethical principle is the pledge by medical practitioners to 'do no harm'. Technologists have long tried to position their developments as inherently neutral and therefore unable to do harm in and of themselves, but only through the way they are deployed. The author Isaac Asimov put this ethical consideration into the realm of technology in his first rule of robotics, which has been generalised as, "no machine may harm humanity; or, through inaction, allow humanity to come to harm". The problem that data brings into this aspect of ethics is that it injects a heavy dose of human bias into the neutrality of the machine, especially in the realm of AI. As examples ranging from algorithms to grade exams that discriminate against poorer students through to photo completion software that assumes most women will be wearing a bikini or low-cut top have shown, the maleficence that happens in human society is all too easy to replicate in automation, leading to potential harms. It is not for nothing that the UK government created the Centre for Data Ethics and Innovation – the issue is clear from its name alone.

4. Fairness

Decisions that are based on data need to be demonstrably fair, both explainable and reasonable. That does not mean an organisation cannot apply its own risk models or acceptance criteria to decisions, provided the basis for these is not unfair bias in data sets. Legislation requires this already, such as the requirement under the GDPR to be able to explain an automated decision or to have human intervention in the process. Being denied access to a product or service is not inherently unfair, assuming there is no potential personal harm from this denial, if the grounds for that decision are fair. A powerful example of how bias can actually be fair can be found in the decision made by the UK government about how to distribute Covid-19 vaccines by starting with the most at-risk groups, even though there are fewer of these in the population. When a critical resource is scarce, fairness demands it be supplied where it will achieve the most beneficence – a good example of how ethical principles are often intertwined.

For this author, there is a fifth ethical principle that also needs to be considered and applied in order for the preceding four to be meaningful, that of sanctions.

5. Sanctions

Medical practitioners found to be in breach of their professional ethics face sanctions, from warnings through to losing their licence to practice. Military personnel can face demotion if they breach codes of conduct. Even footballers can be suspended for a number of games if they receive too many red cards. But data practitioners have no such sanctions, not least because there is no professional qualification or standards board to assess them. Yet unless data ethics come with consequences when they are not followed, they are meaningless. When working out the ethical framework for data that will be adopted within your organisation, thought should be given to what will happen – at an individual, departmental and organisational level – in the event of a violation. Possible options include being moved out of role, a corporate donation to a relevant charitable cause, or a public apology. They should also include retiring algorithms that have been discovered to be unethical, or withdrawing from activities or channels that use biased automation.

Data ethics frameworks

Establishing the principles that underwrite your data ethics is a crucial step which needs to be followed by having them adopted at a strategic level by the organisation. But this is still not the end goal – ethics that only live as statements on a website are empty promises. They need to be lived by everybody in the organisation, underpinning decisions and informing actions.

Just as with data governance, absorbing what this means day-to-day is challenging for data practitioners and data teams, just as much as it is for colleagues across the business. To make this process easier, establishing a framework that makes the connections and dependencies clear can be very helpful. There is a huge number of options for this covering every aspect of data and especially AI, where data ethics get operationalised.

One framework that has gained a lot of adoption and been put into operation was developed by the Open Data Institute (ODI). Its Data Ethics Canvas provides a template for building a practical approach that embeds principles into business practices. The Co-operative (The Co-op) turned to the ODI in 2018–19 when looking to ensure its digital services reflected the values on which the organisation was founded and continues to represent. Table 10.1 shows how The Co-op mapped its specific data challenges onto this canvas, from data rights through to sales procedures.

Table 10.1: The Co-op/ODI Data Ethics Canvas

Data sources Third-party members Salesforce	Data limitations Poor data quality Known bias	Sharing and storing data Who, why, how, where (EEA)	Laws, policies and classification GDPR Confidential Solvency II	Rights over data sources Permission Retail/funeral
Existing ethical frameworks Aligned to Co-op values	**Purpose for using data** Use case Minimum volume Make things better	**Communicating purpose** Channel Frequency Content	**Positive effects** Uplift in member selection of cause Larger marketable base	**Negative effects** Potential for data breach Vulnerable members
Minimising negative impact Reduce harm Measure impact	**Engaging with people** User research, blog, in-store	**Risks and issues** Financial Reputational Regulatory	**Reviews and iterations** Canvas refreshed in beta and live	**What happens next** Actions to close outline support required

This was created through an interactive process using workshops and involving key stakeholders and practitioners, such as digital delivery managers and product owners. Workshops have been developed into a process that allows these delivery teams to demonstrate they have assumed the desired behaviours. At the same time, data specialists are involved to help demystify the data domain for non-technical colleagues.

For The Co-op, this was not just about identifying how data ethics could operate in real-world scenarios – it developed specific products and services via this method. Examples include its Guardian digital funeral service, which required a single source of customer data, personalisation of coupons in-store, and even a shift-tracking app for colleagues. Together with the ODI, the organisation has published its work openly to encourage others to adopt proven practices and has worked directly with Chester Zoo on its own ethical customer data systems development.

Data for good

An extension of data ethics is the adoption of data for good as part of the organisation's vision and purpose. It is widely recognised that data can be used to drive societal and environmental initiatives, from tracking infectious diseases to working on UN Sustainability Goals. Projects like these are beyond the scale and reach of any single organisation and generally require multi-agency engagement. This can happen on a small scale, such as a commercial organisation lending its skills and resources to a charity or NGO – 55.7% of organisations surveyed by DataIQ are running this sort of programme with a specific cause. A higher proportion (58.8%) have joined forces with multi-party initiatives using data to resolve local or global problems, although far fewer (14.4%) engaged with the UK government on its own data-driven activities of this sort. It may be that working with a supra-national agency or cause helps to avoid any perception that data for good has a political dimension.

Examples of data for good activities being undertaken in 2020 include:

- **EDF 'Force for good':** The utility applied data and analytics to ensure that the most vulnerable members of society were given a helping hand. Using a combination of smart consumption analysis and Priority Services data, it implemented various welfare initiatives and mobilised more than 185 smart meter engineers to support energy emergencies, deliver medicine, provide essential meter credit top-ups and, in some cases, even buy and deliver essential shopping to some of society's most vulnerable members during the Covid-19 pandemic.

- **Fields in Trust**: Green space has never been more important for physical and mental well-being and also has an estimated £34.2 billion of value in the UK alone, yet access is not equal across the population. The Fields in Trust organisation created the Green Space Index in partnership with The Co-op to deliver support and intervention to green spaces in the communities that need it most. Its work showed that lower affluent and areas with high numbers of BAME people have the lowest provision, but the highest need.

- **Openreach:** During lockdown in the UK, as people were asked to work from home where possible, Openreach's business delivery team kept emergency services and businesses connected. Its business intelligence team made it easier for engineers to connect the UK's critical national infrastructure, find new and innovative ways to identify critical premises, track the health of engineers and cluster work efficiently. It identified, prioritised and connected 17 hospitals, 198 emergency NHS circuits and over 2,900 other orders for critical services during April and May 2020 alone.

- **Transport for London (TfL):** TfL's transport analytics and data science team is instrumental in providing analysis of travel patterns on the public and private transport network. During the Covid-19 crisis, it provided analysis of traffic patterns to support

TfL's provision of services for the NHS and essential services, and to inform government policy during restricted times as well as restart and recovery phases.

- **Vodafone:** Vodafone has committed to a number of data for good initiatives from malaria epidemiology to helping governments and international organisations deal with the Covid-19 pandemic. By pooling data from all of its markets across Europe and Africa in just eight weeks, it managed to deliver key aggregated and non-personal (anonymous and extrapolated) insights into how diseases spread and how pandemics impact behavioural change. These were used to drive policy changes at a critical time.

The global health crisis has helped to surface the value and impact that can be achieved when data and analytics are applied to problems. It has also revealed the willingness of individuals and organisations alike to have a higher purpose alongside their commercial goals. Data leaders should consider how to leverage this opportunity and where their own resources can best be applied.

DATA LITERACY STEPCOUNTER

Embedding values into the use of data is a core element of data literacy – everybody needs to have a mindset to do the right thing.

Consumers are highly data literate, even if they do not care what happens to their data. This gives data leaders an extra duty of care to consider.

Steps 33–36:

33. Be aware of consumer expectations and anxieties around data usage and build in parameters to new data-driven processes.

34. Be transparent about how data will be used after it has been captured and how customers can control this.

35. Develop a framework of data ethics that reflects the values of the organisation as well as underlying ethical principles, plus what sanctions might apply if breached.

36. Expand the scope of ethical and value-creating data usage into the for good realm to support societal or environmental initiatives.

CHAPTER 11

Becoming
data literate...
and beyond

Advancing maturity

Assessing the as-is state

EVERY JOURNEY STARTS with a single step. When aiming to become data literate or to progress beyond that state, knowing where to place your feet is a good place to begin. That means assessing where the organisation currently stands in its adoption and use of data, how well developed skills are, if data foundations are in place and being used, and whether leadership across all business functions is practising evidence-based decision-making.

A variety of assessment tools exist to measure these dimensions, although many are generic business maturity frameworks that do not necessarily test where the organisation sits on its journey towards data literacy. But data leaders do need a benchmark for their starting point in order to track whether they are effecting change or not – support and funding may depend on showing this.

In research carried out by DataIQ across two cohorts of 196 senior data leaders in end-user organisations, it became clear that data literacy is a work in progress (see Figure 11.1). Even where the level is described as quite high, gaps are identified in different departments. One risk this creates is from political resistance and counter-attacks to the progression towards mature data deployment.

Figure 11.1: Level of data literacy across the organisation

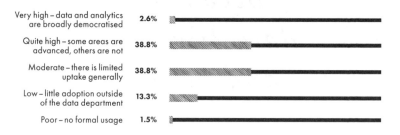

Few, if any organisations, begin this journey from a zero base with no data usage, skills or data foundations of any sort in place. Instead, the starting point for most will be some level of data usage, albeit ad hoc, with few links between vision or strategy and any data function. From this level, however, progress can be significant and even swift.

Maturing from data user to data-driven

Vision – a data leader working in a low maturity organisation needs first and foremost to educate the senior executive about the possibilities that data can deliver. Embracing data as an enabler of corporate goals will kick-start adoption and demand.

Business strategy – if the corporate vision starts to reflect usage of data, then the data leader needs to lay out a clear strategy for how data will come into play across lines of business. At this stage, the first data strategy for the organisation is likely to be created to spell out how this will happen.

Value creation – within the data strategy, opportunities to achieve incremental gains or efficiency improvements need to be spelled out. Business stakeholders may acknowledge any impact achieved, but formal metrics are unlikely to be in place.

Culture – typically, as the organisation moves up to the second level of maturity, stakeholders will begin to make ad hoc requests of the data department. Encouraging this engagement is important, but care needs to be taken about how these requests are managed and prioritised.

Data foundations – making the step up from a very low level of maturity is often where building new data foundations can have the most significant impact. By improving the quality, availability and scope of data, business functions can start to improve how processes operate.

Maturing from data-driven to data literate

Vision – to become data literate, the organisation needs to have widespread access to data and the appetite to use it. Putting democratisation of data into the vision for the business will help to create the demand and conditions for this to happen.

Business strategy – in developing the data strategy, the data leader will translate the business strategy into terms that the data department can support and deliver. At the same time, using positive politics to influence business strategy and ensure it recognises data as an enabler is essential to embed data literacy.

Value creation – one of the biggest steps towards data literacy is the acknowledgement by stakeholders of the contribution made by data in hard financial terms. Even if this is a percentage, rather than a direct metric, it makes value creation from data visible.

Culture – becoming data literate as an organisation without a formal data office is near impossible. Recognising this by appointing a CDO – often the first to inhabit this role – is a key milestone on the maturity path.

Data foundations – having built a core data asset by integrating data silos, the democratisation of data becomes possible. Introducing self-service tools and supporting them with training will ensure that these data foundations gradually become indispensable to business leaders.

Maturing from data literate to data cultured

Vision – that an organisation has a true data culture is most clearly evident in its vision for data, claiming a significant competitive advantage by building towards advanced propositions that leverage data foundations through AI and ML.

Business strategy – data culture is experienced strongly when business stakeholders lay out their strategy in close collaboration with the data leader, engaging from the outset with how goals, foundations and processes can combine effectively and be developed in tandem.

Value creation – every time a new process, product or service is developed that fundamentally relies on data, its owner will establish formal metrics and financial terms for what data is delivered into the project. Data culture accepts that data is not an add-on, but a must-have.

Culture – whatever the reporting line, an organisation with a thriving data culture recognises that the CDO is a significant peer among the senior leadership. Senior executives and business leaders will seek strategic input from the CDO at key decision points.

Data foundations – central governance of data is in place to ensure that democratised data is at the right level of quality and authority. At the same time, advanced projects start to be supported without significant obstacles.

Maturing from data cultured to data native

Vision – data native organisations no longer need to call out data as a component of their vision – it is inherent in everything they are trying to achieve. Indeed, these goals arise out of what data makes capable.

Business strategy – just as the vision is fully integrated, so are strategies in data native organisations. Business stakeholders do not need to explore whether data will be able to deliver what they have in mind – they will know it is already an intrinsic component of the business that they can leverage.

Value creation – putting data on the balance sheet as an intangible asset may form part of the data native organisation's value recognition. Formal financial measures that are recognised by the chief financial officer and reported in the profit and loss account typify being data native.

Culture – a board which contains business leaders who are fully versed in data and assume it will be available, accessible and reliable is one that has emerged from data maturity progression and is now as advanced in its culture as can be. This is likely to remain a future state for most, at least until a generation of digital natives takes over the C-suite.

Data foundations – data never stands still and new capabilities are constantly emerging, not least as technology advances and creates both opportunities and challenges. For data leaders, maintaining the data native organisation requires formal knowledge transfer to keep each part of the business at the same level of maturity.

AND BEYOND...

Data never sleeps, neither does business

Becoming data literate is a realistic ambition for any data leader and the organisation they serve. Others have achieved this state of adoption and usage of data – more can follow their example. Frameworks such as the DataIQ Way provide the roadmap to progress to this level and beyond.

But at the same time, the data leader needs to be conscious of regressive forces that constantly threaten to erode the achievement of data literacy. Some of these are internal, such as political resistance, reorganisation, transformation projects (which may succeed or fail), technology projects that are launched without any involvement of the data department, but which have a significant impact. Similarly, there are external factors that can push back against the adoption of data, ranging from acquisition and merger activity that can undermine a data literate position by bringing a radically different focus to bear, through to market disruption or global pandemic.

Those who bring their organisation to the level of data literacy – or beyond – are to be duly recognised for their significant achievement. Those who maintain this level even more so.

And for those who face starting over or running a recovery programme, remember this – once you have learned the language of data, you can always use it to write a new story.